A NEW CITY O/S

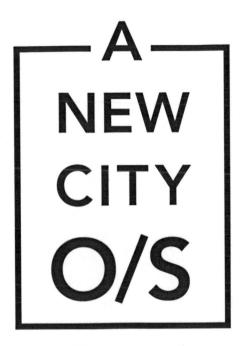

A NEW CITY O/S

The Power of
Open, Collaborative, and
Distributed Governance

Stephen Goldsmith *and* Neil Kleiman

ASH CENTER FOR DEMOCRATIC GOVERNANCE AND INNOVATION
John F. Kennedy School of Government
Harvard University

BROOKINGS INSTITUTION PRESS
Washington, D.C.

Library of Congress Cataloging-in-Publication data are available.
ISBN 978-0-8157-3286-0 (pbk : alk. paper)
ISBN 978-0-8157-3287-7 (ebook)

9 8 7 6 5 4 3 2 1

Typeset in Scala

Composition by Westchester Publishing Services

Contents

For more information, please visit www.anewcityos.org.

Foreword

Steve Case

Each wave of internet innovation produces massive changes in society—in how people produce collective knowledge, entertain themselves, purchase goods, and form relationships. Entrepreneurial leaders, regardless of the sector in which they work, capitalize on these fundamental shifts to drive transformative improvements. But these improvements also pose new challenges: from guaranteeing the safety of autonomous vehicles to making sure new health technologies maintain patient privacy to leveraging the benefits of artificial intelligence. These are the issues the average citizen will have to face in this next wave of innovation—what I like to call the Third Wave. And whether we're ready or not, the Third Wave is here.

In this wave, the role of government will be unequivocally crucial. After all, it will be up to local governments to ensure public safety while adapting to the rapid and vast changes brought about by this new wave of innovation. And historically speaking, the public sector has largely lagged behind the private sector when it comes to embracing new technologies.

There are intriguing exceptions to that rule—new ways cities are mining data for better insights into how to run programs, for instance, and new methods of collecting that data in the first place. But as Steve Goldsmith and Neil Kleiman write in *A New City O/S: The Power of Open, Collaborative, and Distributed Governance*, these innovations are limited by how government is run, not empowered by it.

As the authors suggest, public officials can play an active role in ensuring that this technology wave broadly benefits quality of life—if they can modernize the structure of government. There are many reasons why governance has trailed private markets in incorporating each wave of technological innovation. The biggest, as aptly described in this book, is that outdated structures, immune from the forces of competition, and a bureaucratic culture leave conscientious public employees unable to make service to their constituents a priority.

The Third Wave is already starting to form—even as governance has not fully embraced the opportunities of the first two waves. But that lag is exactly why local government itself is poised to be transformed—there are many, many opportunities for massive change. Officials who follow the lessons in *A New City O/S* can ride this wave of technological change instead of becoming overwhelmed by it.

When I first met Steve Goldsmith in 1999, he was fascinated by the evolution of AOL from a "set of pipes," so to speak, to an aggregator of content designed to improve people's quality of life and break down boundaries—geographic or otherwise—that prevented people with common interests from coming together in everyday life. As mayor of Indianapolis, Steve had been an early advocate of providing city services via the internet, and in 1996, he helped the city become one of the first in the country to make e-government and online delivery of city services a reality.

Several years later, when Steve was chairman of the federal Corporation for National and Community Service (CNCS), he met with my wife, Jean, CEO of the Case Foundation, and again sought ideas centered around the second wave of internet innovation. Jean, as chair of the President's Council on Service and Civic Participation, and I worked with Steve to broaden the ways in which individuals could organize to serve their communities, and the Case Foundation helped CNCS take advantage of social media to engage people in volunteer service. As a result, well before social platforms had obtained much traction in leveraging public goods, CNCS partnered with Facebook to use social media marketing to recruit volunteers for the Martin Luther King Day of Service, coinciding with the day of President Obama's inauguration. The number of volunteers increased fourfold over previous years, soaring to almost 100,000.

Today, the idea of using social media to drive support is commonplace, and yet we're still only on the cusp of what the smartphone revolution can do for local government. What's more, new technologies are continually coming online. Sensor data from wearables, street lights, water pipes, mobile phones, and buildings, for instance, are only part of that Third Wave, and it will give city employees—from health inspectors to urban planners—more and better information than they ever dreamed.

The public sector can learn from the private sector, but it is uniquely different, with its own opportunities and challenges, history, and future. Yet both citizens and the government employees who serve them are frustrated. Citizens see what a responsive large private enterprise can produce for them by capturing the benefits of these waves of technological innovations. However, they don't see similar public breakthroughs. That means they become less trustful of their government, and less willing to become involved or support its programs with tax dollars, voices, and civic participation.

With the potential of these new technologies and platforms for engagement and using data to pre-emptively solve problems, government can produce what *A New City O/S* nicely describes as distributed and collaborative governance that "allows public officials to mobilize new resources, surface ideas from unconventional sources, and arm employees with the information they need to become pre-emptive problem solvers."

The ubiquitous connectivity of the Third Wave will result in breakthroughs no longer produced by a single doctor or researcher, but rather by social interaction with well-curated learning. By moving beyond government's older structures and very tight hierarchies, this model of distributed governance allows employees to both unleash their entrepreneurial spirit and to work across departments with more information and a wider field of partners—including for-profit businesses, universities, philanthropies, and nonprofits. I often cite an

African proverb, "If you want to go fast, go alone. If you want to go far, go together." Partnerships will likely never be more important than they are in this next wave of technological progress.

The *New O/S* captures two principles long important to any work, but particularly useful for government officials:

First, systems need to be designed with a high-quality user experience. Whether acting as a citizen or a customer, anyone will abandon their effort to engage if the experience is not seamless. Having a business owner plow through one bureaucracy after another to open a business is exactly the opposite of where we need to go—and this book shows that.

Second, time counts. For individuals and for businesses. Governments rarely recognize the losses in cost or confidence from slow-moving systems. With Third Wave advancements, government should not only be quickly responsive, but because of the power of big data and sensors, it should be able to solve many problems even before they occur.

In *The Third Wave: An Entrepreneur's Vision of the Future,* I wrote, "We are entering a new phase of technological evolution, a phase where the internet will be fully integrated into every part of our lives." For our government, the internet hasn't been integrated much at all. Our civic infrastructure and our democracy face both critical challenges and amazing opportunities. Steve Goldsmith, for decades one of the country's best-known government innovators, and leading urban policy expert Neil Kleiman, who as a professor at New York University's Wagner School of Public Service and Center for Urban Science and Progress has set the stage for university-city relationships, show how to capture the social power of a more connected system to produce stronger, smarter, more effective cities in this incredibly important book.

Acknowledgments

We express our appreciation to the many people who assisted us in writing *A New City O/S*. First our thanks to the foundations whose generosity supported the research and policy initiatives that animate the book. Kresge Foundation president Rip Rapson, also currently Chairman of the Board of Living Cities, supported our project and is also a critical actor advancing urban revitalization across the country. Chantel M. Rush, program officer with the Kresge Foundation's American Cities Practice, provided keen insights throughout the drafting of the manuscript; and we also received tremendous support from Benjy Kennedy and Carol Coletta.

Patrick McCarthy, President of the Annie E. Casey Foundation, has for decades played a key role in advocating for urban neighborhoods and the children who live in them. We are indebted to him personally and to the initiatives that the Foundation has supported.

Evan Absher of the Ewing Marion Kauffman Foundation provided grant support and invaluable insights for our focus on regulatory reform.

The ideas in this book owe much to previous research and critical analysis of esteemed public management thinkers and experts John Dilulio of the University of Pennsylvania, Donald Kettl of the University of Maryland, and William Eimicke of Columbia University.

We also acknowledge our appreciation to our home institutions. There are so many people at the Ash Center at Harvard Kennedy School whose contributions made a difference. Katherine Hillenbrand, who manages the Data-Smart City Solutions project, provided a tremendous number of ideas and supporting research. Several of the cases in this book first appeared either in the Data-Smart blog or in *Governing Magazine's* Better Faster Cheaper blog. Harvard Kennedy School writers and program assistants Wyatt Cmar, Chris Bousquet, Eric Bosco, Alex Maza, and Monika Glowacki all contributed to those sites and to the book. The Kennedy School–sponsored Civic Analytics Network, which works with talented chief data officers and fellows in many United States cities, also produced content and examples for this book.

Christina Marchand, Senior Associate Director for the Government Innovators Network and Innovations at the Kennedy School, not only coordinated many of the various pieces of this puzzle that resulted in a book but did a wonderful job in managing the relationship between Ash and the Brookings Institution, our publisher.

Many programs and individuals at New York University supported and contributed insights to this book, including the Robert F. Wagner School of Public Service current and former deans Sherry Glied and Ellen Schall; Mitchell Moss, Kathy O' Regan, and Ingrid Gould Ellen, whose passion for cities and ideas of how to improve them was a consistent source of inspiration; Chair of the Department of Population Health at the School of Medicine, Marc Gourevitch; Clay Gillette and Brandon Fuller at the Marron Institute; the Director of the Center for Urban Science and Progress (CUSP), Steve Koonin; Mike Holland and Constantine Kontokosta at CUSP; and Global Research Professor, Richard Florida. A special thanks to Julia Lane, a boundary-breaking collaborator and faculty member at both Wagner and CUSP. Several students and recent graduates assisted with research, including Varun Adibhatla, Yarden Zamir, and Rachel Ginchiga.

We extend significant gratitude to our exceptional editor, Carl Vogel, who for six months engaged with us as a full partner, and whose challenges and questions greatly improved the quality of the concepts.

We each of course thank our families. Steve benefited greatly from a constant exchange of ideas with his wife, Kate, who has an extensive background in nonprofit service delivery and, coincidentally, who served a year as a fellow at Harvard's Advanced Leadership Initiative during the writing of this book, as well as the political input from their six children whose views range from libertarian to leftist! Neil received ceaseless support from the Duitch family: Suri's critical input (and copy-editing); and daily encouragement from Asher and Zelda.

Finally, we each have spent years working with local leaders through-out the world. We have seen the very best of dedicated public servants who make a difference, sometimes against long odds. These heroic in-dividuals keep democracy alive; we acknowledge our debt to them, and the inspiration we take from them, as well.

ONE

The Pivot to a New Government Operating System

The 2016 presidential election ripped away any pretense that citizens are complacent and satisfied with elected and appointed leaders in the United States. Although local and state officials take pride in the fact that trust in local government consistently ranks higher than in the federal government,[1] Americans' faith in government as an institution is shrinking, dropping to 37 percent after the election, even as faith in nongovernment organizations and business increased, according to the highly-respected Edelman Trust Barometer.[2] Moreover, a dangerous trust gap between elites and most Americans is growing. Better-educated individuals who sit at the top of the income distribution reported much higher levels of trust in government than those in the "mass population."[3] With public demands for services continuing to exceed the willingness of people to pay for them—at least when delivered by the current system, which seems impersonal, expensive, inefficient, and distant—that gap will grow.

Fortunately, the societal and technological changes that contribute to heightened cynicism can also power the very transformation of government that will turn much of that cynicism into trust. This book proposes a new model, distributed governance, which pivots away from today's measurements of how well public servants stay on task to, instead, rewarding them for reaching goals that improve the city, turning them from rule-bound bureaucrats to data-savvy problem-solvers. This model pivots from a City Hall that grudgingly doles out information to a platform provider that serves as the hub of city departments and outside partners. It pivots from concern for procedures to, instead, constantly addressing the needs of its citizens. At a moment when cities are, in many ways, asked to do more within an increasingly difficult environment, distributed governance offers transformative operational reforms that will produce better public services, which, in a virtuous circle, will create more citizen trust.[4]

To catch a glimpse of the future's distributed system, look to New York City, which took on the creation—almost overnight—of one of its biggest government programs in a generation: a full-blown educational system to serve tens of thousands of four-year-olds before kindergarten. To build it, the city needed help from a broad array of stakeholders, from families to community centers to IT consultants.

In April 2014 Mayor Bill de Blasio held a press conference to say that the city had put together the funding, with state assistance, to allow New York City to establish a universal program called Pre-K for All, which would offer a seat to every child whose family registered for the program. The plan to help all children get off to a healthy start in life was highly complex, a mix of public schools that would be able to add a Pre-K program for the first time and changes to existing Early Education Centers at schools and community-based organizations across the city, requiring the integration of multiple service areas, actors, and approaches into a coherent whole.

City and education officials succeeded, and more than 50,000 students began Pre-K for All six months after the program was first announced. To get there, New York City agencies and nonprofit partners built a universal Pre-K (UPK) system to identify the right schools, teachers, and students and have them each in the right place, ready to go, by the start of school in September. De Blasio empowered his top aides, including a deputy mayor and a chief technology officer, to work across agencies to reach the goal. The effort involved 500 community-based organizations and other nonprofits, nursery schools, daycare centers, faith-based organizations, and public elementary schools across the city.

Knowing that it was entrusted with the care and education of four-year-old children, the administration assumed the responsibility of being the hub of a capillary system, providing absolute clarity about the basic parameters of the program, such as student academic evaluation. An expedited permitting process ensured without undue delay that each of the sites met health and safety requirements. The Department of Education created a simple and streamlined enrollment process so families could easily apply to programs in district schools or Early Education Centers. To allow parents to make informed decisions on behalf of their children, the city produced information on program quality and created systems to gather data once programs were operational that tracked students, measured progress, and held all providers accountable to basic standards. City administrators knew working parents might need not just a regular school day, but also daycare vouchers, often for a relative to watch their children after the Pre-K day.

With its traditional bureaucratic structure, New York faced mighty challenges stitching together Pre-K for All's disaggregated parts. But the mayor's directive was clear—tight and collaborative organization was essential, and the multiagency working group included such unlikely allies as the Administration for Children's Services (the city's child welfare agency), the Department of Design and Construction, and the Department of Health and Mental Hygiene. Stacey Gillett, the former executive director for strategy and sustainability at the city's Department of Education, remembers:

> It really hit me how well we were working together when there was a press conference and the fire chief stood up and said, "Pre-K for All is my responsibility!" That was amazing and insane at the same time. To know that the Fire Department would do whatever it took to make sure new education providers met safety codes

was what made the whole program work. Everyone knew that failure was not an option and that we all had to work together.[5]

Collaborations also extended to the data and information needed to start up a new education system. Luckily, New York had begun going down the road of data coordination for agencies involving children during the administration of Mayor Michael Bloomberg. Called HHS-Connect, the fledging system provided a starting point, but much of the necessary information remained scattered among an array of city departments, schools, and community organizations. To accelerate this process, the city paired a dozen city agencies with technologists at an all-day Tech 4 UPK brainstorming session for a new outreach platform.[6]

Throughout the process, the city had a user-centric orientation. This may sound trite, but it meant government functioning in a very new and different way. The customer-first approach was most visible in the way officials reached out to parents who were being asked to enroll their four-year-old children in a brand-new program. For Pre-K for All, New York City went far beyond the standard roll out of a new government program, where a program is promoted and then the assumption is people will take advantage of it. Once Pre-K for All was marketed, the real work began. Led by de Blasio's campaign staff, the outreach team knew, just like with a get-out-the-vote campaign, nothing could be taken for granted.

"We just had to go knock on doors," Gillett recalls. She went on to say:

> What made it work were all these 20-something de Blasio and ex-Obama campaign staff working together with us education department bureaucrats. One weekend we needed to canvass citywide and no one knew how we would cover so much ground. Well, one of the young staffers stayed up late, used Google Maps and came in early the next morning with personalized walking routes for everyone. The administrators were [stunned], but it worked.

The same kind of customer-focused attention was paid to the small nonprofit providers. New York City had the daunting challenge of converting hundreds of small mom-and-pop nonprofits and childcare providers into fully certified Pre-K schools. This meant every time there was an issue with filling out an application for fire code safety or to meet specific health standards the onus had to be on government, not the applicant. Administrators—many for the first time—would go back and personally help applicants address any snafus. When many unsafe and unfit providers were eliminated, it was because they truly were not up to snuff, not just because bureaucracy got in the way.

This rapidly built Pre-K system was far from a slapdash effort. Overall, in the first year of operation, 92 percent of families surveyed rated their program as excellent or good, and the entire system continues to enroll tens of thousands of new children every school year. The implementation did bring some controversy; critics charged that the city unfairly required a counterproductive level of process detail from out-of-favor charter school providers, making it impossible for them to participate.[7] Yet on the whole, Pre-K for All has worked better than most traditional service systems.

How did this overnight system come together so well? Because in the rush to tackle a major issue at scale, the city was forced to develop a distributed system that is customer-focused, has the speed and flexibility to find partners who could advance the effort, and gives those partners significant downstream autonomy, with nearly complete data sharing driving the entire system. And at the center, the city provides standards and guides teachers, curriculum, and overall systems operation with clear directives.

DISTRIBUTED, INNOVATIVE, AND OPEN

The hallmark of distributed governance is openness that supports deep and real communications, coordination, and connections across City Hall and a broad range of third parties, including residents, contractors, community organizations, local institutions, and nonprofit and for-profit organizations. In this model, the city serves as a hub for the civic work of these entities and its own agencies, leaving behind the strict rules and tight control of information that retards innovation and collaboration. By turning outward, cities can raise their trust and legitimacy in the eyes of residents, augment their data with more and better information to make smarter decisions, find new partners to deliver specific services in more efficient ways, and hear about and collaborate on exciting and new approaches to addressing urban challenges.

Establishing distributed governance will require a new operating system (O/S) at City Hall: a major reframing of public sector operations. For a smartphone or laptop, the O/S is the platform that supports the device's basic functions and allows different applications to run, regardless of whether they were created by the company's software engineers or an outside vendor. It is the underlying system that becomes noticeable to the user only when it isn't doing its job well.

The hardware, software, and cultural infrastructure of the new city O/S will allow multiple parties to concurrently speak, listen, and learn about matters important to the quality of life in a community. Local government, in this new model, engages residents, employees, and external partners dynamically through a connected web that produces knowledge while enabling all the nodes in the system to be more effective on behalf of the common civic agenda.

What distinguishes disorganization or even a loosely connected ad hoc network from distributed governance is a socio-technical ecosystem that organizes information, its role illustrated in figure 1-1. The "technical" aspect of this ecosystem mines and integrates data from a wide range of sources then analyzes and presents the information in a way that is suited to support outcomes, share information, and serve administrative systems that support those who do the public's work. The "socio" aspect is the new relationships, protocols, and expectations that create a collaborative, problem-solving approach. The new O/S is dedicated to constantly designing better user experiences for both the public and the employees tasked with supporting them and to "acting in time"—working at a speed that allows for preemptive problem-solving, concurrent processing, and a culture that values the time of residents.

Even the scale of New York City's UPK success—with so many innovative elements working in concert—is still all too uncommon. Decades into the computer age, cities simply haven't modernized enough. Although this book is not about technology, it recognizes that technologi-

FIGURE 1-1   *Elements of Distributed Governance*

DISTRIBUTED GOVERNANCE
New government model based on open communication,
coordination, and connections in and outside of City Hall

NEW O/S (OPERATING SYSTEM)
The operating system that supports and
enables distributed governance

Building Block: Acting in Time	Building Block: User Experience	Building Block: Socio-Technical Ecosystem

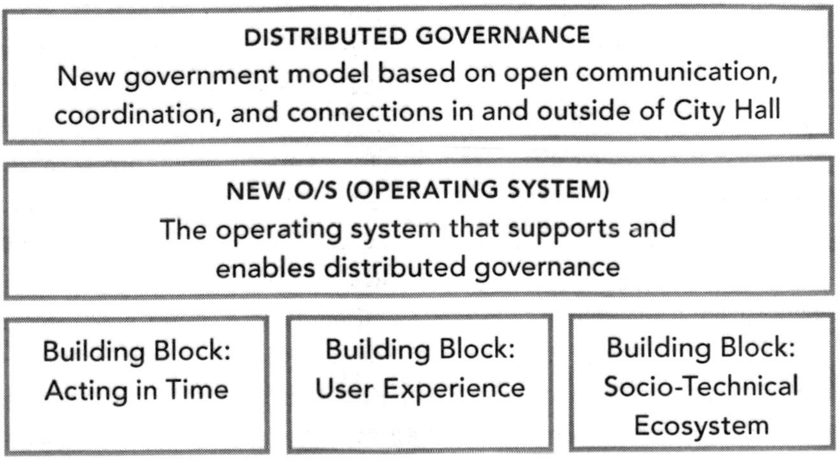

cal changes force, enable, and power the transformation to distributed governance and a new O/S. Amazing tools now provide promise to frustrated citizens and civil servants; mobile and cloud computing, GPS, data mining, digital platforms, and more could be harnessed to create radical new ways of delivering municipal services and running city government, if only we would let them.

These technologies have revolutionized the private sector, even for "old economy" firms like Caterpillar (CAT), a company that has been manufacturing heavy-duty equipment for a century. Today Caterpillar embeds sensors in its equipment to monitor fuel efficiency, idle times, engine performance, and location. Through a partnership with the sophisticated data scientists at Uptake, a Chicago-based analytics company, Caterpillar transforms massive amounts of daily data from those sensors into insights that optimize fleet operations with predictive analytics that allow operators to repair equipment before it breaks, reducing downtime and improving results.

The current design of government originated in the same era as industrial companies like Caterpillar, and a few principles from the company's transformation can serve as signposts for cities. CAT had been accruing large amounts of data from its assets. The company was able to make the most of a network system when that data savvy group worked with CAT to design tools that helped improve its employees' capacity to do their jobs. According to Caterpillar executives, its work-force moved from a system based on responding to failure to one based on anticipating and solving problems. Data analytics and a new way of operating unlocked the industrial giant's capacity to have more informed mechanics, a new mission for its work, and more satisfied customers.

There are many examples of cities across the United States applying new innovative technologies. In Minneapolis, sensors on bridges now tell the city when the structure needs attention, and in South Bend, water pipes send a message to authorities when a change in water pressure signifies a problem. By mining social media messages, food inspectors in Chicago change their schedules and resolve problems more quickly. In New Orleans, data helps fire department officials determine which dwellings are most at risk and should receive a free smoke alarm. Los Angeles residents can use open data maps to see how the response times for basic city service requests in their neighborhood compare to other parts of the city, and agencies use the information to coordinate street cuts and repairs.

We know these changes and more are happening because we've seen them. We have crisscrossed the country, evaluating and writing about new urban practices in partnership with Living Cities, and a num-ber of philanthropic organizations, including Bloomberg Philanthro-pies, Annie E. Casey, Kresge, Ewing Marion Kauffman, and Laura and John Arnold Foundations. The insights and quotes from experts involved with case studies and examples throughout the book are culled from our notes and interviews from this work.

What we haven't seen in local government, however, is the kind of change that happened at Caterpillar. Rather than spreading across de-partments, these inventive urban efforts typically remain lightning in a bottle. Hundreds of exciting new programs and initiatives dot cities across the country, but no one city has found a way to mainstream these approaches fully into day-to-day activity. Obsolete laws and rules and a culture dominated by red tape and narrow discretion stand in the way of a system that rewards collaboration and results.

The O/S we envision includes crucial new information from new hardware such as sensors and mobile devices, analysis of this information and data from other sources, and wider availability of solutions from cloud-based software. Just as important, it also includes revising the internal code of laws, rules, and structures that makes public services tick. It values employees who solve problems over those who follow a routine, who collaborate with rather than manage residents, and who work across sectors and departments rather than labor in shuttered silos.

Note that this book has a focus on city government, but often uses the phrase *local government* in its place. The concept of distributed, open governance is not solely meant for cities—its capacity is just as applicable at the county level and for other units of local, and in many instances state and federal, government. We believe that forces of customization, collaboration, and speed that have proven transformative in the private sector can energize public sector workers once these rules change.

THE PROS AND CONS OF MUNICIPAL BUREAUCRACY

The current operating system of American cities is more than one hundred years old. The bureaucratic model today is the same as was championed by a powerful political movement designed to reform corrupt urban political machines, as epitomized by New York's Tammany Hall, that incorporated favoritism, nepotism, and wildly unaccountable spending. There is no exact date for the establishment of the current municipal operating system, but many scholars associate it with what was dubbed the Progressive Movement, which took hold in the United States before 1920. One of the first Progressive governments dates to 1900, when Galveston, Texas, recovering from a terrible hurricane, created a "commission" form of government, with appointed professional administrators empowered over an elected mayor. Hundreds of other cities followed with similar commission governments, and New York City famously implemented the nation's first large-scale civil service system in 1913, headed by Robert Moses before he took on the mantle of master builder.[8]

Led by business and citizen groups, the Progressives created an entirely new professional model that incorporated formal civil service exams, job classification systems, and procurement rules that were eventually codified into many state and city charters and laws. No more hiring your cousin for the construction job. Procurement would be centralized and operated within a heavy set of regulations. To reduce bribes and other abuses of building inspector discretion, cities created hierarchical supervision that ensured adherence to rules and uniformity of practice.

Progressives built their systems for government in line with the era's foremost management philosophy, referred to variously as scientific management, Taylorism, and, most aptly, Fordism, after the assembly lines for Model Ts created by industrial pioneer Henry Ford. They believed government, like automobile manufacturing, worked best through relentless dedication to mechanization and efficiency. The sociologist Max Weber described the bureaucratic model as built around "fixed and jurisdictional areas which are generally ordered by rules" supported by "trained experts" who have the authority to give the required commands.[9]

The operating system designed to support that approach professionalized municipal service and reduced risk, both to the municipality and to its employees, by enforcing uniformity. Reforms in the Progressive era worked in many ways, stamping out most patronage and leading to greater fiscal integrity and reliable city services such as routine trash pickup and street maintenance. The movement even indirectly led to the creation of the two schools of administration where we teach—the John F. Kennedy School of Government at Harvard and New York University's Robert F. Wagner Graduate School of Public Service—each of which opened during the Depression to train the new managers called to fulfill the Progressives' vision.

For many reasons this then-effective model of yesteryear no longer works so well. The public expects government to do far more today under much more complex and interconnected circumstances than was expected a century or even fifty years ago. Cities today have taken on a large measure of responsibility, from job growth and economic mobility to environmental sustainability and drug abuse issues, that a mayoral administration was not expected to have an answer for in 1927. As urban responsibilities grew, cities' systems added more departments and job titles, becoming more fragmented along the way. A child living in public housing will not have the full opportunity he deserves, even if the family receives multiple services, when the teachers, caseworkers, and counselors in his life do not work in an integrated way, with shared information and coordinated interventions. As well, unlike a half-century ago, third parties—nonprofit and for-profit contractors—today provide a broad range of services that exercise the will of the state outside of the government's informational or personnel systems.

It's not just the system that is too siloed; professional officials' peripheral vision can be limited, as well. Promotion up today's public-sector organizational ladder requires employees to develop specialized technical skills; the resulting professional culture and training can be so insular that public servants develop blind spots to other, better, ways to address a problem. Take law enforcement. Have the training and metrics we use to prepare and evaluate police officers made them too narrowly focused on arrests? Has that played a part in soured relations with residents in some minority or low-income communities? And, in the end, do these issues help or hinder the ultimate goals of less crime and increased public safety on the streets?

Certainly, creating programs and operating a city in today's complicated world in no way resembles building a car nearly a century ago. After generations of adding new limitations on workers, the very rules designed to frustrate graft and waste now also frustrate employees who "are continuously monitored and investigated by auditors, judges, budget examiners, performance evaluators, legislative committees, public watchdog groups, clientele associations, citizen bodies, and media organizations eager for a good scandal."[10]

Absent an outcome-based orientation, city departments now promote fidelity to work rules and risk avoidance over measurable accomplishments. Current operating systems devote great amounts of energy to monitoring rule compliance while largely ignoring the cost in time and money of doing so—and often ignoring the actual results of the activities, as well. Compliance is an easy activity to measure, but it comes at a price. When employees are evaluated on how carefully they follow rigid rules, they can infuriate citizens with clearly inapplicable questions or approaches, misapplying the city's time and effort. The number of structures that have been inspected may seem like a logical item to track, but each building does not represent an equal fire risk, just as all restaurants do not pose the same health hazard. It certainly is challenging to define specific outcomes and even more difficult to address how to achieve them—particularly with the analog approach of years past—but without it, city bureaucracy is limited in its capacity to truly serve the public.

Finally, the Progressive structure cannot easily deal with today's distributed nature of information itself. Nearly thirty years ago, Francis Rourke of John Hopkins University wrote, "The specialized knowledge that Max Weber once saw as the comparative advantage that bureaucrats would always enjoy in debates on national policy is now much more widely distributed through American society."[11] Government systems developed when bureaucrats owned and controlled data. Every day residents now use apps and social media to solve problems and monitor public decisions, often by accessing publicly available data. They shop for products that have been customized exactly as they want, using online systems with a minimum of transactional friction. These voters/consumers know that the size of an enterprise is no longer an excuse for red tape, long lines, delayed processing, or lack of responsiveness.

Add it up, and what does the Progressive model typically look like in the twenty-first century? Take the solid waste division in Memphis, responsible for solid waste collection, recycling, composting, and dead animal collection services across the city. We use this example in part because, in chapter 5, we will explore how they successfully addressed the troubles outlined here. Before those innovative solutions, however, the division was facing big trouble. The system, with a staff of 454 and a $58 million annual budget, had gotten to a point where it did not reward employee performance, operations expenses exceeded private sector benchmarks by a large margin, and the department's weak retirement system induced older workers to stay on the payrolls even when ailing. Fleet services charged the department internal expenses that unnecessarily raised costs and weren't clearly presented to or understood by the city council or department leaders. As finances worsened, the department fell further and further behind in adapting new technologies that could improve services. A lack of data and performance reporting had gotten to the point where no one even knew the number of vehicles in the fleet or how much the staff cost.

With all these problems coming to a head, city and union officials faced off in a lose-lose contest of wills. According to management expert Skip Stitt, who consulted with Memphis on the issue:

> The union leadership discharged its responsibilities of fighting for its members while the managers did theirs by fighting on behalf of the mayor and council to get more productivity out of the workers. In a system where only a few people had access to information, neither "side" really trusted the other. In fact, the top-down process, by both the union and management, caused them to miss the bigger picture, that archaic routes and bad fleet repair practices harmed everyone.

For too many city managers, employees, and citizens, the situation Memphis faced sounds all too familiar. The processes and programs that were the pride of the Progressive era now often choke innovation and efficiency from our cities.

It is important to note that the new O/S does not ignore or glide over the troubles that launched those Progressive reforms. Corruption, patronage, and waste still lurk. The open governance and increased employee autonomy that are hallmarks of the new O/S can produce better results for these ills, too, compared to closely held information and tight, managed hierarchies. The tradeoff between discretion and accountability for civil servants, which underlies most current public-sector management, can be replaced with a better balance, as well as accountability defined more in terms of outcomes.

This is possible, in large part, because new digital tools provide much better capacity to truly manage those who spend the public's resources or utilize public authority. With GPS, managers can know where their field employees are working and how long it takes to do the job. Resident engagement tools and photos from the workers themselves on their mobile devices could let managers see if a project is complete and done well. To comb for evidence of bias, machines have the capacity to read field notes and documents written by officials who work directly with the public. Data analytics can identify outliers from restaurant or building inspectors who write too many or too few violations or spend too little or too much time at an establishment.

In other words, the goals of the Progressive system stand tall. But the method of getting there is now more than obsolete—it's become counterproductive and should be replaced with a new, engaged public employee armed with better information, but also better managed, trained, rewarded and, indeed, where necessary, better disciplined.[12]

TODAY'S BEST PRACTICES ARE NECESSARY BUT NOT SUFFICIENT

A few years ago, while deputy mayor in New York City, Goldsmith held a breakfast meeting with a dozen neighborhood leaders and local small business owners in a modest, three-story walk-up office building across the street from a small park. Quickly the conversation turned to the torn-up park, barricaded from use due to construction that had been started and then seemingly abandoned. Time and time again the breakfast partners pointed out the window and complained that the park had been unusable for almost a year.

Later, when pressed for an explanation, city officials confirmed the story but defended their actions as compliant with the laws. Twice they selected the lowest bidder for general contractor services, even though these bidders presented bare minimum qualifications. Both times the contractor's incompetence became clear after the contract was awarded, leading to termination. The procurement shop had accomplished its goal. By following the process to find the lowest bid to the letter, they avoided getting sued but produced a truly awful result: a park hidden for months and months behind construction fencing instead of filled with children playing and parents talking about the fun and challenges of raising kids.

Now imagine a collaborative and open governing model where neighbors play a central role in the park's redevelopment. As parks officials scope out ideas they present them on easily used, interactive online tools where children, neighbors, and leaders can not only add comments but work with the display software itself to produce examples of alternative or improved ideas. The city, conscious of the cultural and financial circumstances that can limit the use of online communication tools for some of its residents, has designed a community feedback system that builds participation that fairly reflects the entire neighborhood at this and each stage of the project's development.

Once a crowd-sourced, expert-reviewed plan is ready, the city mines data to rate the quality and timeliness of bidders for the work, reviewing past projects that those bidders have done to understand every aspect of their capacity and performance. When the plans are developed and the construction award made, neighbors armed with smartphones and SMS texts report to city and community websites every day about the conditions they observe—the city learns when there are issues that need its attention without relying on or awaiting a visit from a city inspector. Resident documentation of shoddy work becomes part of the record should the contractor bid on other public projects. The city's cameras stream pictures of the work site, and neighbors supplement the video with their uploaded pictures. Every aspect of the renovation is open, enhanced at each stage by a collaborative process and involved residents.

Because residents were involved with initiating the design and connected to the construction, many of them become interested in volunteering for programs in the new park and to help with the gardening, as well. New vibration sensors installed by the city tell officials when equipment needs maintenance before it hurts someone, and sensors in trash cans report when it is time for pickup. The wireless infrastructure provides citizens in the park with free, high-speed Wifi services. The park, for many reasons, now truly belongs to the community.

This is a hypothetical scenario, but there are slivers of this new O/S right now taking shape in many cities across America, as some highly effective mayors, supported by philanthropy and driven by new technologies and involved citizens, produce breakthroughs. Ted Smith embodied this new and inventive approach when he was the innovation director in Louisville, Kentucky, for five years, beginning in 2011 with the election of Mayor Greg Fischer. Smith is a high-energy, fast-talking official whom you might mistake for a corporate consultant (which he formerly was). He likes to say that he created his innovation list by looking for shortcomings in Louisville. "Everyone has their 'best of' lists. So, the chamber of commerce will tell you about job growth and how we are home to the Kentucky Derby. Well, I'm the guy who looks for the 'worst of' list," he says.

With that line of thought, it didn't take Smith long to realize that in Louisville, worst includes air quality. Nestled in the Ohio River Valley, the city often fills with hot and humid air, trapping pollution. By any measure, the region ranked near the bottom of environmental assessments, always making the top ten lists for worst particle pollution and receiving failing grades from the American Lung Association.[13] At the time, Louisville's asthma rates were far higher than most cities, and the city's corporate recruiters struggled to explain the terrible air conditions to businesses thinking of relocating.

Given air quality's impact on quality-of-life and economic development, Smith had the full support of the mayor to devise a solution. But when he called the local health department, it wasn't interested. The agency, while well run, had its own priorities, like the spread of opioids. There was also a commonly held belief that not much could be done: the city was in a valley, for better or worse. Smith tried something different. He called David Van Sickle, previously a researcher at the Centers for Disease Control, whom he knew from his days working in the Obama administration. Van Sickle had come up with the ingenious idea of using tiny GPS devices affixed to pocket-sized asthma inhalers and started a company (Propeller Health) to commercialize it. When a sufferer needed to use the inhaler, it sent a signal to the main database. With the collected data, researchers could better understand localized air quality and its link to health.

Smith took the idea and went to three local philanthropies to fund a pilot project with several hundred residents, which led, two years later, to a major grant from the Robert Wood Johnson Foundation to cover the costs of buying and distributing more than 1,000 inhalers throughout Louisville. The results were stunning. After reviewing and geocoding the data, Smith and his team could pinpoint the worst locations for pollution, as well as the worst time of day and part of the year. They were surprised to find that some of the most asthma-burdened parts of the city were not near factories (as most suspected) but a few miles downwind. Now the city is using these insights to mitigate the damage, with such measures as planting more "biofilters" (tree and shrub combinations) in highly polluted zones and, especially, near congested roadways by schools. The entire process was relatively cheap, too, as technology costs have tumbled. For far less than even a typical environmental review, the city has been mapped for air pollution impact in real time.

This book's quest for a new operating system features many innovations like what Mayor Fischer, Smith, and his team accomplished in Louisville with a potent recipe of data, public and private partners, and a focus on creativity and outcomes. Yet this book is not about simply innovating. On the contrary, completing a specific innovation through a dedicated group can mask the fact that enduring, rigid systems continue to undergird municipal governance. In fact, many exciting innovations have succeeded only because private foundation funding and special initiatives allow cities to avoid existing government processes and systems.

Maybe the biggest lesson from Louisville's innovation was that it was all done as a "work around" of existing government structures. Since the public health department remained a bystander, Smith set up an independent nonprofit, the Institute for Healthy Air, Water, and Soil, to give the project a home. "We had a remarkable innovation on asthma and public health issues, but we had to create an entirely new nonprofit to get it done," Smith says. "So, for about two years I had my government job *and* I was executive director of this new nonprofit."

Innovations are flourishing in many cities and counties, driven by an innovation delivery team or by piloting a creative new technology. This book puts most of these new urban innovations in the category of "project innovation"—advances in addressing a problem but without much impact on larger government systems. In a sense, these current innovations occur in a parallel universe while the traditional government enterprise continues to hum along virtually undisturbed. These advances often succeed because they avoid entanglements with government agency rules and processes rather than reforming them.

In our work, one of the most common accomplishments we hear about involves getting around an entrenched bureaucracy. One local official told us, "The moment I move my innovative project to HR or the budget office, it's over." Much of this has to do with a phrase Anthony Downs coined, the "law of increasing conservatism," which "posits that bureaucrats will clinch on to rules to minimize risk and punishment for errors."[14] From a purely technical point of view, bureaucratic government can attain a high level of efficiency[15] yet still seem unresponsive and frustrating to its citizens. As David Beetham at the University of Leeds wrote in the book *Bureaucracy*, "An organization whose operations are highly routinized may be very cost-efficient, but for that very reason be incapable of responding quickly to some sudden and unexpected change in the environment."[16]

BUILDING BLOCKS OF THE NEW O/S

The key to understanding and then implementing distributed governance is one word: *open*. Government organization and approaches need to fully recognize the change from closed, professionally directed systems to open, participatory ones. Most cities in the United States today adopt open data approaches. But true open governance recognizes that valuable information and good ideas originate broadly and need to be shared. When government operates as a *platform*, to use a term originally referenced by Tim O'Reilly[17]—with information pouring in from citizens, Internet of Things (IoT) sensors, official observations, government partners, and other sources—it can no longer run using the tightly closed set of procedures of the Progressive era.

The movement from closed to open sweeps across all aspects of governance. Previously, planning was the exclusive domain of professionals. Now it can be done with cloud-based design modeling tools available to communities. It used to be that the mayor announced the budget and angry residents could complain when it went to committee. Now some cities are starting to experiment with open participation in the budget-making process. In the closed system government gathered performance information on paper and eventually compiled the results

FIGURE 1-2 *The New O/S Pivots City Government*

INTERNAL SYSTEMS PIVOT:

- From daily activities defined and limited by agency rules to openness to new opportunities and cross-agency collaboration

- From compliance measures to impact measures

- From a top-down enterprise to one that empowers public employees as problem-solvers, armed with data, deserving of discretion, and with the capacity to make decisions

EXTERNAL SYSTEMS PIVOT:

- From vertical governance where City Hall is a monopolist of information and responses to a platform provider of networked solutions

- From government organized for its own convenience to one that puts the citizen front and center

- From the central producer of public value to an integrator of contributions from a wide swath of external entities

to show what happened the previous year. Now sensors and residents' smartphones pulse information in and out of government every second of the day. In an open-asset model, government and its citizens can not only know where their garbage trucks are at all times, they might be able to convince the city to share the trucks for a community cleanup.

Open systems require not just better government but better governance, where City Hall sets rules that protect its citizens while facilitating solutions that involve nonprofit, for-profit, and community partners. Alexandru Roman of California State University San Bernardino nicely summarizes open systems theory when he notes that "all organizational dimensions are interrelated and interdependent, which means that shifts along any one aspect will echo throughout the system."[18]

An open environment requires governance to protect public values even while expressing less concern about who owns the assets or responsibilities associated with delivering a solution. Government, of course, has responsibility for privacy and security protections, but information generated from thousands of different sources "is no longer defined or contained as a discrete entity of a well-defined system but becomes more flexible and mobile as it is processed in and across a variety of systems and applications."[19] Trust, integrity, and accountability all depend on how easily information can be digested and utilized.

The Flint water contamination disaster, for instance, was borne of multiple government blind spots and poor decisions over the course of years. Alex Salkever, in *TechCrunch*, asks if it would have been prevented if the State of Michigan and federal government had requirements that all data be open and machine readable, writing, "We cannot and should not rely on the government to always keep us safe. This is not an indictment. Governments are fallible, just as any other large organization is fallible. But 100 years ago, there was no way to easily access, analyze, and monitor government activities. Today, there is no excuse not to do so."[20]

In distributed governance, *open* goes even further than outsiders monitoring government—it is about these entities participating and partnering with it. Solutions to issues confronting cities are knit together across an open system that has seamless borders between sectors. Today's government bureaucracy trains professionals in a discipline and then provides them with information available only to City Hall to make policies and design operations—lower-level employees are asked to mechanistically and uniformly implement the assignment under tight supervision. Distributed governance redefines professionalism as being prepared for open information and open boundaries, ready to develop knowledge and plans socially from many sources through sharing data and proposals, and then implementing a multi-sector solution.

To reach this distributed governance, cities need a new O/S, an entirely new system, that deeply incorporates shared information, trusted social networks, and structural changes that give them the capacity to set roles and rules for conduct, quality, equity, and privacy for participating partners (see figure 1-2). Public officials will need the personal and technical skills to allow them to concurrently listen to and create information in a system where legitimacy and authority will often be mashed up across partners.

The Progressive era model for governance is based on mechanization and uniformity; it achieves this with a bureaucracy's tight supervision that respects hierarchies and a culture of following rules. The model of distributed governance is based on openness and collaboration; it achieves these goals through a new O/S that is built from three core building blocks, each of which is shaped—and, indeed, even made possible—by the last decade's massive changes in technology and the new expectations and capacities those changes have wrought. The building blocks work in concert, each providing support and greater capacity to the others. Below we highlight these building blocks for a new O/S, which we will explore in depth in the chapters that follow.

UX: Government Designed with the User in Mind

In the tech world, UX stands for user experience design—making a product or process easier to use, access, and enjoy through how one interacts with it. As a building block of the new O/S, UX controls how government interacts with residents and with those who deliver public services to them. City departments have, in large part, designed their systems for their own convenience, usually from the top-down specifications of a senior official or because government approaches its responsibilities with an agency-driven, vertical orientation. But that has it exactly backward. Systems, services, and programs should be designed around the convenience of the key users. A human-centered approach uses well-visualized and contextualized information to redesign physical and virtual experiences.

City Government That Acts in Time

The new O/S needs to support speed: in operations, service delivery, regulations, and planning. *Acting in time* in this model is more than a minor goal of tightening response times to resident requests. Cities can make velocity a priority and fundamentally change how they operate with predictive analytics to identify and intervene in situations before problems occur. Machine learning can free up employees from mindless, routine paper shuffling, and facilitate synchronous processes which allow public sector workers to organize and deliver coordinated solutions quickly. Cities can use data and social media to identify and mitigate true risk while freeing up business owners with good track records to build their houses or open their restaurants more quickly and at less cost.

The human and technical skills exist to deliver much more responsive services to residents, which, in turn, will improve our cities and strengthen our communities. Government can go from being methodical to rapid, from reactive to predictive. City departments can change from being oriented around agencies' needs to an orientation toward citizens' convenience supported by systems and policies that will have the most impact, with performance measured by outcomes rather than activities accomplished. City staff can stop working in vertical silos and become collaborative and flexible.

A Socio-Technical Ecosystem for City Hall and Beyond

To create distributed governance, where citizens, their public servants, and significant external partners work together to establish better outcomes for the community, City Hall must build a socio-technical ecosystem that includes both administrative changes and enhanced digital platforms. Data mining tools allow officials to take information from many sources: from multiple departments within City Hall, from organizations working with the city, and from residents posting on social media or participating in structured outreach sponsored by the city. The city and other partners can then integrate, analyze, and present that information, now more valuable from its breadth of scope, its context with other data, and from being examined by algorithms that offer new answers and opportunities.

Yet a deep embrace of open governance is not solely about software and hardware, as important as these elements are to its success. The administrative systems supporting the current bureaucratic system are relatively straightforward—procurement, human resources, IT, and the like that supposedly help government discharge its responsibilities in an accountable way. The administrative structure of distributive governance needs to change how it supports the public employee as a knowledge worker. The new O/S values public servants who use data to inspire new questions about how the city operates. This culture of innovation requires the right people with the right training, which means changes in HR and procurement departments, whose procedures and approaches often impede getting the right person or contractor engaged.

This socio-technical ecosystem has profound impacts for both public servants and external partners, explored in depth in chapters 5 and 6, respectively. The system redesign acknowledges that most civil servants will enjoy the workday much more when they can avoid counterproductive rules and nonresponsive internal administrators and concentrate, instead, on making their city a better place to live. At the same time, the new O/S offers unprecedented avenues to listen to citizens, organizations that contract with the city, and local institutions to incorporate their ideas into creating a better city.

WHY NOW?

People have been complaining about how hard it is to get someone at City Hall to listen to their problem—let alone do something about it— for a long, long time. So why is now the time for a new O/S? There is more than one answer.

We have no choice. The challenges facing America demand action now. Frustration and distrust threaten community cohesiveness, at times spilling into violence and protest. Social media tools and around-the-clock news flashes amplify grievances. Society, communications, private companies, and individuals have all changed their behavior. For the most part the structure of government has not. Increasing complexity in the delivery of services and the interconnectedness of public problems demand new, integrated approaches that involve a bureaucracy that listens and responds more broadly and effectively.

The digital revolution sweeping through society and the private sector provides new opportunity. New technologies can change every aspect of City Hall—the capacities of public employees and how they are hired, trained, and managed; procurement; performance evaluations; and more. New analytic platforms allow government to vastly increase not only efficiency but customization and citizen engagement in ways not conceivable even a few years ago.

Pervasive open data broadly empowers society. Residents can freely access and interact with open data from their cities, communicating with the government and others interested in similar causes. If their government isn't keeping up, it seems even less relevant or trustworthy. But if utilized correctly in solving problems and communicating results, this very openness becomes a key asset. An operating system that continuously delivers high-quality and responsive services, where residents, workers, and managers easily interact with their government, observing what is working and what is being accomplished, can help develop the necessary levels of trust that support democratic governance.

Recent innovative breakthroughs produced by local leaders across America have created momentum for change. Despite the structural obstacles they face, creative public leaders have been producing innovations that prove that government can unlock a new era of excellence. Weaving together the new tools and a range of project innovations and combining them with a new approach to governance will allow not just project innovations but enterprise-wide responsiveness.

Universities and foundations are becoming increasingly relevant resources to drive insights and changes in local governance. New ideas for public policy and data-oriented efforts are being developed at universities throughout the country. At the same time, local and national philanthropies have become increasingly committed to supporting local government improvements. Until a few years ago, even foundations that invested in U.S. cities in large part limited their grants to 501(c)3 nonprofits that addressed urban issues. Now there is a growing recognition that much of our future prosperity will be dependent on solving the formidable challenges that cities face.

Major changes in governance rest at our fingertips. Government now has access to the same technology that has pried open so many previously closed systems, instantly knitted together massive amounts of information, and allowed individuals to communicate with friends on their own terms and to shop for almost anything under the sun from their bedroom. Yes, much work is required. The implementation guide in the appendix lists ten notable challenges to establishing a new O/S, as well as actionable recommendations for overcoming those hurdles. But a new era of distributed governance will allow public officials to mobilize new resources, surface ideas from unconventional sources, and arm employees with the information they need to become pre-emptive problem solvers. Today's public-sector leaders have a better opportunity to make dramatic advances in the quality of the services they deliver than at any time in the last century.

Chapter 1   **THE BOTTOM LINE**

Key Points

■ A hundred-year-old operating model for local government impedes broad-based reforms. The surge of urban innovation around the country usually requires a "work around" of obsolete laws, layers of regulation, and a compliance-at-all-costs culture.

■ The new O/S pivots from a closed and professionally directed system to an open, participatory one that takes data from many sources, including sensors, residents, and partner organizations, and organizes it in a way that enhances the user's experience. The new system is not just about hardware and software, but also involves reworking the internal code of government rules, laws, and structures that make cities run.

■ While not a technology fix, the new O/S is informed and fueled by technological advances, including customization, collaboration, and speed.

Pitfalls

■ While it is common to believe that all current municipal reform is rooted in technological advances, that is only part of what can and must be done to build a new operating system.

■ Do not assume that citizens' trust in government can be won back solely with a few notable reforms.

Recommendations

■ Do not underestimate the challenges of moving to distributed governance, as this is about systemic and systematic reform: rewriting the code of government.

■ Look for clues to the new O/S in current innovations.

Examples

■ With an urgent and ambitious goal of establishing a new service for 50,000 preschoolers, New York City established a governance structure for a distributed system: clear safety regulations set by the city, standardized curricula, parental input and choice, and multiple educational providers from government and nonprofit institutions—all connected with a digital backbone and defined by speed, flexibility, and customer service.

NOTES

1. Gallup, "Trust in Government," 2016 (www.gallup.com/poll/5392/trust -government.aspx).

2. Edelman, "Trust and the U.S. Presidential Election," 2017 (www.edel man.com/trust2017/trust-and-us-presidential-election).

3. Edelman, "Edelman Trust Barometer," 2017 (www.edelman.com /trust2017/).

4. OECD, "How Better Governance Can Help Rebuild Public Trust," 2017 (www.oecd-ilibrary.org/governance/trust-and-public-policy_9789264268 920-en).

5. This and all future quotes are from personal interviews with the authors, unless otherwise noted.

6. Susan P. Crawford and others, "On the Road to Pre-K for All: The Launch of UPK in New York City," *Berkman Klein Center for Internet and Society Research Publication* (September 2015), p. 24.

7. "Mayor Pre-K Stiffs Success; Universal Education for Everyone except Those Unions Don't Like," *Wall Street Journal*, June 9, 2017.

8. Dennis Judd and Todd Swanstrom, *City Politics* (New York: Routledge, 2015).

9. Max Weber, *Economy and Society: An Outline of Interpretive Sociology* (University of California Press, 1978), p. 650.

10. Charles C. Goodsell, *The Case for Bureaucracy: A Public Administration Polemic* (Washington, D.C.: CQ Press), p. 120.

11. Francis E. Rourke, "American Bureaucracy in a Changing Political Setting," *Journal of Public Administration Research and Theory* 1 (1991), p. 120.

12. Stephen Goldsmith, "Progressive Government is Obsolete," *Wall Street Journal*, March 18, 2011.

13. American Lung Association, "State of the Air," 2016 (www.lung.org /assets/documents/healthy-air/state-of-the-air/sota-2016-full.pdf).

14. Anthony Downs, *Inside Bureaucracy* (Boston: Little, Brown, 1967).

15. Weber, *Economy and Society*, p. 223.

16. David Beetham, *Bureaucracy* (University of Minnesota Press, 1987), p. 22.

17. Tim O'Reilly, "Government as a Platform," in *Open Government* (Mountain View, Calif.: Creative Commons, 2010).

18. Alexandru V. Roman, "Counterbalancing Perspectives on the Current Administrative Telos of American Bureaucracies," *Administration and Societies* 26 (August 2014), p. 12.

19. Michael P. Crozier, "Governing Codes: Information Dynamics and Contemporary Coordination Challenges," *Administration and Society* 47, no. 2 (2015), pp. 151–70.

20. Alex Salkever, "To Prevent Another Flint, Make All Open Data Machine Readable," *TechCrunch*, February 18, 2016 (https://techcrunch.com /2016/02/18/to-prevent-another-flint-make-all-open-data-machine-readable).

TWO

The State of Innovation

What We Have and What We're Missing

In Washington, political and policy debates rage, but cities primarily implement. Of course, there are politics and disagreements about priorities and programs, but most elected officials and their voters rightfully believe there is no need to fiercely engage in partisan battles around ideology at the local level. In our experience, most local officials are "doers"—admirably focused on identifying key issues in their cities and trying to find the resources and solutions that can make a difference. As New York City's former mayor Fiorello La Guardia quipped, "There is no Democratic or Republican way to pick up the trash."[1]

Over the last few years, street-level government has begat some of the most inventive policy in America precisely because the trash has to be picked up even when the budget is getting squeezed. There is no shortage of fresh approaches, and cities big and small around the country are advancing literally hundreds of new programs, strategies, and technology-driven initiatives. We have been among the many advocates for this renaissance, writing about urban reform, judging innovation competitions, speaking at conferences, and providing hands-on technical assistance to cities advancing creative policy and program reforms.

New websites, podcasts, and policy publications have been launched to cover this rise of new ideas, some funded by a wave of venture capital from leading private philanthropies. For example, the Annie E. Casey Foundation has made substantial investments in municipal innovation. The Laura and John Arnold Foundation has funded advances in operational excellence, data, and enhanced criminal justice, and Living Cities, a consortium of leading foundations, is providing resources for technical support and collaboration among city leaders. All four of the major local government associations—the International City/County Management Association, National League of Cities, the U.S. Conference of Mayors, and the National Association of Counties—have working groups on either innovation or new technology approaches.

As noted in chapter 1, this book dubs most of these advances *project innovations*. They typically improve services, sometimes in an impressive manner. When it comes to more systemic change, though, ad hoc innovation can give the illusion of widespread progress, distracting time and attention from the more difficult and broad-based need for structural innovation. Worse, officials may look at an innovative accomplishment and think, instead, that they are seeing an innovative enterprise that is prepared for twenty-first-century governance.

That said, it is important to try to get a handle on what, exactly, we mean when we talk about project innovation. A thorough literature review finds few texts that assess the current wave of local innovation (Sandford Borins and Jorrit de Jong being two of the exceptions).[2] Most policy reporting—including our own—has been descriptive in nature, often detailing program elements rather than critically assessing new innovations or placing them in a larger context.

The remainder of this book discusses the elements that constitute distributed governance and the new O/S, but this chapter will take the measure of where municipal innovation and governance efforts are today: What is the existing foundation on which something new can be built? Provided here is a broad summary of current categories of project in-

novation and an exploration of the evolution of one of the seminal theo-
ries of city government relevant to a new O/S.

ASSESSING THE CURRENT INNOVATION LANDSCAPE

To really understand what can be unleashed through a robust new
urban O/S, it's critical to have a solid grasp of the state of the art of municipal project innovation. Any attempt to create a compilation of project innovations in cities nationwide will not be exhaustive, and we are
not necessarily endorsing any specific program that fits into one of these
categories. But it is useful to clarify the current state of play. These innovations provide important elements of the new O/S, illustrating components that need to be built into and applied broadly across government
to establish distributed governance.

Project Innovations: Innovation Teams

Forming a team dedicated to finding new solutions to vexing urban issues sounds so simple, but innovation teams are a relatively new addition to the local government landscape. More than any other municipal
innovation, these teams embody core attributes of the new O/S: clarity
around ambitious new outcomes, speed, and a core focus on empowering and unleashing the creative ideas that often lie dormant within city
agencies and among residents.

Innovation teams are often a small interdisciplinary band of data,
design, research, and project management pros aimed at some of the
highest-level and most complicated city priorities, such as lowering the
homicide rate, devising a climate action plan, or addressing persistent
poverty. These special teams are usually comprised of individuals drawn
from the private and public sectors, serving as something akin to internal
consultants. In the past eight years, the concept has caught on, going
from a handful of locations to sixty-six cities in the United States in 2016.
Bloomberg Philanthropies has provided the greatest support for the concept, making grants totaling about $50 million to several cities over the
past five years.

Innovation teams have shown impressive results. The Memphis Innovation Team created a new model for providing small business assistance through a framework called "clean it, activate it, sustain it," shorthand for a series of interventions such as improved street lighting, pop-up and rent-free retail space for local entrepreneurs, and creative reuse of historic properties. The team targeted commercial strips in economically distressed neighborhoods and showed real improvement; in two communities, vacancies were reduced by 80 percent and new business license applications increased by more than 10 percent from 2012 to 2014. In Louisville, an internal agency competition led to an expansion of citywide recycling. And Chicago's innovation team eliminated redundant regulation and overly burdensome business licenses by 60 percent, saving local employers as much as $2 million annually.

Because they are not bogged down in day-to-day operations, one of the virtues of innovation teams is flexibility, and they tend to take on a range of issues: homelessness one year and juvenile crime the next. A few cities have formed notable domain-specific teams, as well. The Rockefeller Foundation has funded twenty-three U.S. resilience teams that focus exclusively on environmental and sustainability issues, for instance, and in New York City mayor Michael Bloomberg created teams dedicated to specific subjects, such as the Center for Economic Opportunity, which was focused squarely on reducing poverty.

To create their new processes innovation teams depend on strong relationships with city agencies. With a mandate of crosscutting and cross-agency change, the teams can authorize new approaches to addressing an issue, but they must first get information and buy-in from the people who will be implementing the plans. Smart innovation teams know that when it comes to a press conference to announce the new plan the frontline workers and their managers deserve to stand front and center.

Yet when it comes to wider impact, the greatest shortcomings of innovation teams come from one of their biggest strengths: they are outsiders. Because the team is external to municipal budgeting structures, organization charts, and operations, they almost never have an impact on them. An innovation team can accomplish great things for a city, but when the project is over—and external funding is expended—cities still need to fully integrate the approach.

Some cities have started to address this issue of how to get innovation teams to spur wider impact. "We had some great innovation team success but now are trying not to have innovation labeled as the 'cool thing,'" says Rebecca Rhynhart, former chief administrative officer of Philadelphia. "We don't want innovation to occur at the fringes of the bell curve. In the past, the innovation folks were on the edges of how the city runs and not changing the core of how the city functions." In a handful of cities, including Atlanta and Louisville, which began with support from Bloomberg, the administrations have both maintained their innovation teams and started to explore how to make more fundamental changes to core operations.

Project Innovations: Data and Technology

Some data-driven ideas are substantive in terms of powering how a city operates and the impact on the lives of residents. Others are bright, shiny objects—they help solve a specific problem but don't have the kind of fundamental power required for far-reaching change. Here is a quick take on the current state of play.

(Citi)Stat

CitiStat stands alone from all other data-based reforms for its duration and the number of cities and agencies that have adopted the model. Stat (that is, statistics) programs establish a routine process to hold agencies accountable for performance by presenting data benchmarked to specific goals in areas from crime reduction to park cleanliness. CitiStat, the city-level program, is modeled on CompStat, a policing program initiated by New York City Police Department Commissioner Bill Bratton in 1994 to measure how well bureau chiefs and officers were accomplishing various crime-fighting goals.[3] With CompStat, police departments use data to determine precisely what kind of crime is on the rise and where, and then require commanders to devise strategies to bring those numbers down.[4]

Using data to measure performance in this way is now widespread in cities big and small. For example, Boston publicly tracks and publishes metrics on everything from crimes by neighborhood to on-time trash pickup. Many of these stat programs are now attempting to incorporate new data analytics tools into their processes. Analytics allow performance teams to predict the causes of problems rather than just responding after they occur. Incorporating more sophisticated analytic tools will also assist cities in a shift from measuring narrower activities to more systemic issues; for example, looking at homelessness rather than simply the number of shelter beds.

Citizen Response Apps

With mobile devices nearing ubiquity, many cities have developed instantaneous citizen response platforms, often supported by SeeClick-Fix, a social enterprise that allows residents to just snap a photo of something the city needs to repair, such as a broken streetlight or gaping pothole.[5] The responsible city agency gets a new work order and the message sender automatically gets a note back saying exactly when the issue will be resolved. Other interactive apps allow residents to text in queries, such as asking about the closest bus stop or subway station.

In 2017 more than 250 local governments had adopted such a citizen response application. It's not hard to see why chief executives around the country have made them so popular so quickly. They give residents instant satisfaction and a concrete sense of what the city will be doing—and when. Essentially a new pact is formed with citizens, as they can ping government anytime and are promised an immediate response.

This helpful breakthrough does not come without unintended consequences, however. "My mayor insisted we adopt this response platform, which is great on the front-end with residents. But we did nothing to change the back-end—the guts of how we work to fill potholes and meet other requests. So, we had the same slow response time as before and [layered on top of that] new citizens requests coming in, so in the end we went backwards in terms of speed," one city administrator told us. In Boston, Chief of Streets (and innovation team cofounder) Chris Osgood notes, "I am a big proponent of the you-call-we-respond culture. However, if it is the sole way of managing operations and prioritizing investments, it can pull focus away from more long-range and underlying issues—in effect pulling us away from being truly responsive."

Open Data and Transparency Movement

In the context of government, the open data movement refers to a relatively recent policy movement based on the concept that since the public technically owns the vast amount of information possessed by government, that information should be readily available to the public, subject to policies on security and privacy. The Sunlight Foundation has highlighted seventy cities that, through council legislation and mayoral edicts, instituted open data policies.[6] The movement has unlocked a veritable treasure trove of municipal datasets.

In Las Vegas—one of the most open governments in the United States—all it takes to learn about crime statistics, construction permits granted, or lobbyist activity is access to the Internet. With open data even some CitiStat performance information has moved from a closely guarded secret to being available to all. And whether viewing restaurant scores in San Francisco or flu outbreaks in Chicago, the public can not only view the data but also use it to create maps and apps that compare data over time and across communities.

Yet open data isn't as easy to use as it could be. In most cities, the agencies that release the data don't provide the information visualized in a useable way, organized thematically, or geographically tagged. Abhi Nemani, once a proponent of open data when he worked for Code for America and as the former chief data officer in Los Angeles, said, "I think we moved too fast. There was this mass dump of data but no process to use it. The issue is we don't have the systems, infrastructure, or platforms to translate any of it. So really open data is only open if you can do something with it."

Smart Cities and the Internet of Things

There is probably no more confusing label in the data tech field than *smart cities*. We have heard countless mayoral aides bemoan the day their mayor came back to the office convinced the city needed to become *smart,* with little sense of what, exactly, that meant or how to do it. We will eschew the specific term and simply describe the activities cities engage in when aiming for the smart moniker: They deploy sensors that work in concert with data generated by residents and public employees, curated and analyzed in a manner that improves official understanding of patterns in critical operational and policy areas which, in turn, enhance the effectiveness of personalized services.

Through what is commonly referred to as the Internet of Things (IoT), city departments can gather real-time data from trash cans, lightposts, bus stands, and other street infrastructure. The connectivity of these "things" to the Internet, when deployed well, can optimize operations into better public service delivery: cleaner streets, cheaper maintenance routines, improved ambulance routes. For example, ShotSpotter data from sound sensors guides police to where a gunshot occurred, and license plate readers detect stolen vehicles.

The definitions of what exactly falls into the category are still fuzzy, but more important, there are relatively few places comprehensively utilizing IoT innovations. There are a few notable pioneers. Chicago, with its Array of Things, uses sensors to gather air quality data. Sensors in Syracuse and South Bend make sure water pipe and fire hydrant pressure is adequate, and in Indianapolis a parking meter informs the city that it is out of service before a disgruntled motorist calls to complain. Information from smart streetlights and kiosks presents significant opportunities, but so far cities don't have an organizing platform to connect information or a very deep and comprehensive way to use it.

Big Data

A possible runner-up to smart cities in the misunderstood category is *big data,* which has become the catchall term for using large administrative datasets to improve city services. Government organizations effectively deploy data mining, sophisticated analysis, and visualization to understand massive amounts of municipally generated data. With terabytes of Medicaid data, patterns of criminal conduct, 311 reports, transit routes, and employment information, mixed and matched, analysts can see trends or predict events.

Big data is often defined by the four Vs: volume (mass amounts of data), velocity (correlations drawn in seconds that in the past would take years to see), variety (aligning dozens or hundreds of datasets), and veracity (big data is often far more accurate than traditional statistical methods). Several cities now have an entirely new job category, data scientists, on the payroll to handle big data. In Los Angeles, for example, a mobility manager now analyzes data from taxis, Waze, transit, and private automobile patterns to help manage transportation in underserved areas.

At the basic level, big data is not much different than traditional social science; it's about correlation and prediction (for example, assessing whether closer proximity to farmers' markets leads to lower rates of diabetes), except that today's IT world has unleashed vast amounts of computational power, along with dramatic reductions in data storage costs and increased access through cloud-provided software. Several critical efforts are at the forefront of municipal big data, such as the project being led by Rayid Ghani at the University of Chicago, who is using data analytics to predict which police officers are more likely to abuse authority so they might be counseled before committing an infraction.

As exciting as these efforts sound, most cities are at the very beginning stages of incorporating big data strategies. Hurdles include significant privacy issues and, most important, the fact that even rudimentary predictive analytic efforts require both data science expertise and accurate data—something few local governments possess. Some of the best work is occurring where cities have formed strong partnerships with universities and other intermediaries that can provide analytical capacity.

Project Innovations: Rethinking Standard Operating Procedures

This category covers the new ways of improving how cities accomplish basic yet crucial government operations, such as budgeting, financing, and program design. For generations city government has followed the same basic rules, but options now exist that can save cities money, make them more responsive to citizens, and/or speed up procedures.

The most promising initiatives are exciting to consider, though many are experimental and none widely adopted.

Participatory Budgeting

Municipal budgeting is notoriously secretive, walled-off with little input from government stakeholders other than the most senior leaders, let alone resident involvement beyond rote testimony at long budget hearings. Participatory budgeting turns this model on its head and says residents have full discretion over a small portion of the budget. The effect can be transformative for government-resident interactions.

Participatory budgeting has played out exceedingly well in locales that have tried it, such as New York City where council members engage residents. Community members band together to research and assess needs, then vote on which projects will receive the allotted funds. The process has served as a proof of concept of how seriously and effectively genuine citizen participation can be built into municipal government. But at this stage only a small handful of communities have embraced the approach, and even there the process is applied to an exceedingly small slice of the budget pie. In New York City, for example, fully thirty council members now dedicate 20 percent of their capital discretionary budgets for community control. Although that totals $40 million dollars per year, it's less than half of 1 percent of the city's $80 billion budget.

Pay for Success

Municipal procurement can be looked at as an opportunity to purchase results, not just commodities and activities. Under performance-based contracting, government forgoes tracking of short-term outputs (such as the number of people in a job training class) to focus on whether or not specific goals are met (did the training class lead to gainful employment). This approach began to take root throughout government in the early 1990s.[7] In effect, these contracts transferred the risk associated with paying for services (and not getting what was being paid for) from government to the contracted provider.

The most current form of this idea is a model called Pay for Success (PFS). The PFS approach (sometimes referred to as *social impact bonds*) provides a novel, no-risk way for government to fund new and innovative interventions. Typically, a government agency enters into a multiyear contract for services with a private organization, agreeing to pay for the services only if they result in agreed-upon goals that have been negotiated at the beginning of the contract period. An independent evaluation is conducted to certify that outcomes have, indeed, been met.

Under PFS, a third party, typically a private investor, takes on the risk associated with the contract in exchange for an opportunity to earn a profit. In concept, government is able to pay for the investor's return because positive outcomes will lead to less government spending in the future. For example, if a number of participants in a social service program for at-risk youth avoid becoming enmeshed with the criminal justice system for three years after being enrolled, the city will be able to save money on policing and prison expenses. If specific, defined targets or goals are met then the investor recoups the initial outlay plus an agreed-upon return. If the goals are not met, the investors incur the loss. One of the larger projects of this kind is taking place in Chicago, where city leaders have reasoned that full-day pre-kindergarten for low-income families will significantly boost kindergarten readiness and third-grade literacy. The city is converting 2,600 half-day Pre-K seats to full day with the support of a $17 million bond backed by Northern Trust, Goldman Sachs, and the J. B. and M. K. Pritzker Family Foundation.

The Pay for Success model is still relatively new; the mechanism was launched in England in 2010, and it can take years to truly determine if a program has succeeded. The first major U.S. effort in 2012 was a bold, new program aimed at reducing recidivism among sixteen- to eighteen-year-olds detained at New York City's Rikers Island, which for various reasons did not meet its goals. Partly because of that effort, many new bond-funded projects reduce some of the complexity while still firmly pointing toward pay for performance.[8]

Nudges to Behavior

The term *nudge*, as it refers to government action, was popularized by University of Chicago economist Richard Thaler and Cass Sunstein now of the Harvard Law School in *Nudge: Improving Decisions About Health, Wealth, and Happiness*.[9] Their theory, based on behavioral economics, argues that individuals can be prodded with the right cues to pursue a behavior that is good for the individual and/or for society. To date, nudge use has been straightforward: requiring calorie counts on menus, writing letters in a way that encourages parking tickets to be paid sooner, texting a woman to remind her of a prenatal visit.

The private sector uses such behavioral insights all the time, from just the right image on a postcard from a vacation rental company to the carefully chosen words in the description of the benefits of a mortgage loan product. Only recently have government agencies gotten in on the approach. The U.K. government established a highly successful nudge unit that, with just a rewrite of an explanation on driver's license applications, saw the number of individuals who signed up for organ donations skyrocket. The U.K. unit was spun off from government into a nonprofit organization with a global focus, called the Behavioral Insights Team, which received Bloomberg Philanthropies support to develop a North American team that now works with many U.S. cities.

In New Orleans, city officials working with the Behavioral Insights Team use nudges to improve property maintenance. Formerly, when a 311 complaint was made about a property, the city would inspect the property to see about the alleged problem. Now when an issue is raised, a letter is sent nudging the owner to remediate the problem that led to the complaint, which in many cases causes the owner to proactively take steps to fall into compliance. In these cases, when the inspector arrives, there is no longer a need to levy a fine and start an expensive legal process, saving the city money and the homeowner trouble.

THOUGHTS AND THEORIES TOWARD A NEW O/S

The systemic impact, if any, of the specific innovations in the categories just described on government operations is not entirely clear. As Joshua Franzel, of the Center for State and Local Government Excellence, writes, "In the mid-twentieth century, researchers often empirically tested factors that encouraged innovations used by the federal, state, and local levels of government. From the 1990s to the present, however, few have carried on this tradition of investigating innovations."[10]

However, there is one well-thought-out theory about government outcomes that helps cities and their advocates understand both how to measure the impact of project innovations and what elements to include in building a new O/S. This framework focuses squarely on results in government and is commonly referred to as New Public Management (NPM). Advanced in the late 1980s and early 1990s, and powered, in part, by the seminal book, *Reinventing Government* by David Osborne and Ted Gaebler, NPM is often summed up with the glib phrase, "doing more with less."[11] The idea is that by approaching government in an entrepreneurial fashion; using detailed data as an accountability mechanism; and applying the most current business management techniques, such as increased competition and customer satisfaction surveys, government can provide much better services—without necessarily allocating additional funds. Indeed, NPM thinking has inspired many improvements in government, including successful public-private partnerships, one-stop centers for disparate government services, and an increasing focus on the performance stat systems that track and benchmark a wide array of services.

In recent years, however, NPM has been criticized by civic leaders and academics as fostering an "accountability regime" and subjecting public administrators to answer to narrowly defined goals and numbers. Scholars, including Carolyn Heinrich from the University of Texas, note that NPM has led to a high-stakes environment in which administrators game the system; some government agencies have even been found to distort numbers to reach target goals.[12]

Even without fraud in the system, administrators and staff—facing strict rewards and sanctions based on the data—can focus too much on the activities measured by the metrics (for example, teaching to the test). In these cases, the benchmarks themselves distract officials and workers from addressing more fundamental and underlying issues. Writing in *Governing* magazine about NPM-type reforms, John Buntin found that many inventive public officials opposed a strict NPM approach because it sapped creativity. Some characterized stat meetings as devolving into "dog and pony shows that focused on polish[ed] presentations rather than cycles of experimentation." Kristine LaLonde, the former innovation director in Nashville, said in this article, "The department heads I have the most respect for hated it the most. People didn't trust the system."[13]

Even apparently straightforward metrics, such as potholes filled, create distortions. If the real goal is a smooth street, then repeatedly fixing the same pothole (and counting it every time) is counted as an accomplishment, rather than determining the underlying cause of why it keeps occurring at that spot and addressing that cause. A focus on outcomes, not outputs, should be inherent in any program informed by NPM, but over time—in part because outputs have been much easier to measure—many cities have used the NPM ethos in this incomplete way.

New Opportunities and NPM

Although NPM has weathered a fair amount of criticism, many cities still support and are working to improve programs inspired and informed by its framework, and observers have seen improved government service as a result (often these kudos come from the same critics).[14] There is a recognition that, done correctly, it is a good thing to have government focus on efficiency, data-informed decisions, and services that are more responsive to citizens. In recent years there has been some excellent conceptual thinking about how to improve and build on NPM reforms. In his practical guide to improving NPM, *Trying Hard is Not Good Enough*, Mark Friedman discusses a need to focus on the people served by government. "Profound differences exist between programs and populations," he notes, and the NPM approach must incorporate a focus on the people actually affected by government programs.[15]

Far from castigating NPM, we argue that the *Reinventing Government* movement made invaluable contributions. In fact, Goldsmith eagerly applied NPM principles in programs he promoted as mayor of Indianapolis and deputy mayor of New York City. For a new O/S, NPM is an important step in an evolution of public management.

A few years after *Reinventing Government*, John Dilulio's edited book *Deregulating the Public Service* provided a compelling academic argument for bureaucratic reform by challenging the many ways in which rules limit government reform and effectiveness, particularly in personnel and procurement.[16] In that book Dilulio argues that the current system prevents officials from using common sense and discretion. Scholar and management expert Don Kettl adds that, "the boundaries across which government, its programs, and its officials must work have become far more numerous and infinitely more complicated," thus requiring more flexibility and fewer rules.[17] Ten years after Dilulio's deregulation advocacy, Goldsmith and William Eggers presented a framework in *Governing by Network* that posited that innovation solely inside the four walls of government would never be sufficient to meet citizen needs.[18]

We believe these reform advocates got most of the equation right: the importance of focusing on results through an entrepreneurial drive to improve coupled with more flexibility to work across agencies and institutions. However, when these ideas were published, technology had not yet advanced to the point where it had the capacity for massive change that is now possible, and the scholars worked within the confines of the existing operating system.

Even well-established municipal technologies that have been used as tools for programs informed by NPM have changed mightily in just the last five or ten years. CompStat originally used pins on a map and notebooks filled with government-produced data (not notebook computers; notebooks). Today, police supervisors have almost instant access to a broad array of data, and stat preparation includes hyperlinks and analytic tools. Data mining, cloud computing, social media—these technologies can be the basis of a more distributed, collaborative governance and vastly more accountable employee discretion. Think about what the work life of today's sanitation and street worker could be like. His truck can be GPS enabled, and his smartphone has the capacity to give him a diagnosis of a mechanical problem once he types in a few symptoms. He could arrive at a worksite prepared because a broken streetlamp already sent in its problem, or because a resident sent in a photo, and the maintenance official has ready access to detailed information about the electrical grid and prior repair issues. Today's public service worker can be a problem-solver in real time in a fashion not even dreamed of before.

One excellent scholarly article by Jeremy Millard notes that new technologies mean that government can do more with more, not more with less.[19] More data—big data—can be mined readily and easily, and to make sense of it we need more frames of reference—including more contextualization and a granular understanding of how the results of policies and programs are, in part, shaped by race, class, and geographic location.

Related to but distinct from new technology opportunities, the new O/S will also enable officials to rethink how they evaluate success, holding city government accountable for results that go beyond what is currently measured. In an activity-based government, the goal was to keep input steady—or lower it—and increase outputs. Take, for example, homeless services. A homeless agency will have inputs of allocated revenue, employee time, and the number of shelters it manages. Outputs will be the number of homeless people housed by the agency or receiving doctor visits.

An outcome can include less street homelessness or the number of citizens who leave homelessness for a better life. With more nuanced, deeper data and a focus on collaborative governance, cities can hold themselves accountable for outcomes—not the measures that serve as a stand-in for the goal but the goal itself. This level of accountability can't be achieved with a smattering of project innovations. Cities must embrace a full, new O/S, with the building blocks that are described in the ensuing chapters, to make this leap.

Chapter 2 **THE BOTTOM LINE**

Key Points

- City-level officials have ushered in a new era of experimentation and innovation, focusing on program and service improvements rather than getting caught up in partisan debates.

- The wave of project innovation has been fueled, in part, by private philanthropy, which has made more direct grants to cities.

- Innovation teams have been a vanguard of innovative municipal government. Their status as outsiders has helped power their ability to make bold suggestions, but cities must sustain the team culture for consistent and enduing long-term impact.

- New data capacity and approaches allow innovation and accountability to be measured more by results than inputs.

Pitfalls

- Do not mistake project innovation (improvement in a specific area) with enterprise innovation (systemically reforming core government functions). Cities have often achieved remarkable project success by "working around" traditional public sector administrative systems.

Recommendations

- When taking on or evaluating innovation it is critical to apply an outcome-based framework, starting first with what value the agency intends to create and then proceeding to a definition of which inputs can produce that value.

- New Public Management's focus on detailed data and accountability is a good starting point for distributed governance. But rather than take a "do more with less" approach, the new O/S does more with more—more data, technology tools, and partnerships with civic and business actors.

Examples

- Innovation teams composed of a small band of project management pros have proven that cities can address big challenges by combining data, creativity, and attention to ideas that often lie dormant within city agencies.

- A number of relatively new approaches—social impact bonds, behavioral insights, and participatory budgeting—have shown that traditional government operations, such as finance and program design, can be rethought in bold new ways.

NOTES

1. The Economist Explains, "Why Has New York Voted for a Democratic Mayor?," *The Economist*, November 7, 2013.

2. See Sandford Borins, *The Persistence of Innovation in Government* (Brookings Institution Press, 2014), and Jorrit de Jong and Sanderijn Cels, *Agents of Change: Strategy and Tactics for Social Innovation* (Brookings Institution Press, 2012).

3. Teresita Perez and Reece Rushing, "The CitiStat Model: How Data-Driven Government Can Increase Efficiency & Effectiveness," *Center for American Progress*, 2007 (www.americanprogress.org/wp-content/uploads/issues/2007 /04/pdf/citistat_report.pdf).

4. Bob Behn, *The Performance Stat Potential: A Leadership Strategy for Producing Results* (Brookings Institution Press, 2014).

5. See SeeClickFix (https://en.seeclickfix.com/how-it-works).

6. See Sunlight Foundation, "Open Data Policy Collection" (www.open datapolicies.org/browse/all).

7. Joseph Gayeski, "Towards a Performance-Driven Social Sector," *Third Sector*, 2016.

8. Nicholas Bergfeld, David Klausner, and Matus Samel, "Improving Social Impact Bonds: Assessing Alternative Financial Models to Scale Pay-for-Success," *Harvard Kennedy School Mossavar-Rahmani Center for Business and Government*, September 2016 (www.hks.harvard.edu/sites/default/files/centers /mrcbg/files/Final_AWP65.pdf).

9. Cass Sunstein and Richard Thaler, *Nudge: Improving Decisions About Health, Wealth, and Happiness* (New York: Penguin Group, 2009).

10. Joshua Franzel, "Urban Government Innovation: Identifying Current Innovations and Factors that Contribute to Their Adoption," *Review of Policy Research* 25 (2008).

11. David Osborne and Ted Gaebler, *Reinventing Government: How the Entrepreneurial Spirit is Transforming the Public Sector* (New York: Penguin Group, 1993).

12. Carolyn J. Heinrich, "Outcomes–Based Performance Management in the Public Sector: Implications for Government Accountability and Effectiveness," *Public Administration Review* 62, no. 6 (2002), pp. 712–25.

13. John Buntin, "25 Years Later, What Happened to 'Reinventing Government'?," *Governing*, September 2016 (www.governing.com/topics/mgmt/gov -reinventing-government-book.html).

14. Gouxian Bao and others, "Beyond New Public Governance: A Value-Based Global Framework for Performance Management, and Leadership," *Administration and Society* 45 (May 2013).

15. Mark Friedman, *Trying Hard Is Not Good Enough* (Santa Fe, N.Mex.: FPSI Publishing, 2005), p. 8.

16. John J. Dilulio, *Deregulating the Public Service: Can Government Be Improved?* (Brookings Institution Press, 2011).

17. Ibid.

18. Stephen Goldsmith and William Eggers, *Governing by Network* (Brookings Institution Press, 2004).

19. Jeremy Millard, "Open Governance Systems: Doing More with More," *Government Information Quarterly* 32 (August 2015).

THREE

UX

Placing Citizens and Those Who Serve Them at the Center

The user experience (UX) stands at the center of the new O/S. From Silicon Valley to New York City, tech companies pay close attention to how the public or their clients use their product, what makes it easier to understand or more fun to play, because they know that UX will control the success or failure of a website or an app. For cities, the users are residents or the public employees who serve residents, and the experience includes all the ways in which a citizen interacts with or receives information from government: websites, mobile devices, water bills, kiosks, charts at community meetings, phone calls with a call center, signs at an office.

In a distributed system, the city focuses on UX in part to build trust and improve resident participation. Cities presently provide services in an era with two very strong undercurrents: political polarization and a media and communications world that is both more wide-ranging and more targeted than ever before. Trust in government is falling across the board.[1] For cities to gain trust they need political capital, and that will only come from a pivot to more responsive and competent governance. To paraphrase philosopher John Dewey, if the mayor is going to call the public together to accomplish something truly important for the community, it needs to be done on a foundation of trust and confidence. Geoff Mulgan, in his book about public sector strategy, notes:

> Today the most valuable things that democratic governments want to grow are intangible like trust, happiness, knowledge, or competent institutions. . . . Trust creates trust whether in markets or civil societies. Knowledge breeds new knowledge. And confident institutions achieve the growth and societal success that in turn strengthens the confidence in institutions. Much of modern society is about setting these virtuous circles in motion, whether through investments and programs or by creating the right laws, regulations and institutions.[2]

UX plays a critical role in creating a community sense of pride and cohesiveness. Every time a citizen interacts with government—regardless of whether it is in person, on the web, or through an experience with an employee or contractor—it builds or erodes his or her feeling that the city is fair, competent, and open to ideas and partnerships. Building the political capital necessary to undertake important projects requires a dramatic improvement in the day-to-day experiences residents have with local government.

When city data is accessible, well-designed, and curated, citizens who have more faith in the city are more willing to become involved with efforts for the public benefit, and improved UX can help them use that data to build momentum for change among other citizens. With the interactive nature of today's technology, they can provide feedback and open discussions with each other and with city leaders. The city can help translate those communications from the noise of crowds to wisdom through a good UX that helps organize the discussion and motivate understanding and participation.

Cities also communicate loudly by how they deliver services. The bureaucracies designed by Progressives adopted strict rule-driven processes to thwart ward heelers who, in their own ethically challenged manner, put the politically well-connected at the forefront of their "community engagement." The reform rules essentially said to a citizen, if you want government help, here are the routines you follow, along with everybody else. There was no app, no online process—just a line in which you stood. Officials today need to adopt an omni-channel approach, rejecting the concept that the public should be pleased to receive government services no matter how difficult the experience. Citizens deserve the right to choose the best channel for them, and officials should relentlessly focus on citizen satisfaction.

This chapter addresses UX in three ways. The first two are about the relationship between City Hall and the citizens of the city. The user experience should be paramount to the design of how homeowners get building permits or the design of an app intended to provide information to residents. Slightly different, but as important, is how government creates a discussion thread to inform its discretion around an issue or question—for example, presenting data about river quality in a way that assists environmental groups in their policy development and advocacy.

The third type of UX in this chapter is for public employees: How can the city best communicate with field workers and city partners so their user experience allows them to be more effective in serving the city? A public employee induces trust by problem-solving and needs the tools to do so. In the new O/S, where public employees move from compliance to an outcome definition of accountability, workers need access to good, easy-to-use information to solve constituent problems.

WHEN GOVERNMENT USES UX

Major industries in our economy—banking, retail, healthcare, hospitality, manufacturing—have access today to huge amounts of data, with increasingly complex and powerful tools to analyze the information. UX for companies in these fields is a crucial part of their business

model because it determines how end users—like store managers, hospital administrators, and financial advisors—receive that data and analysis
to best do their jobs, and what customers see and learn, as well. Companies pay close attention to which datasets are included, how the information is presented, and how to measure its impact. They know that if
complex data leads to a complicated or muddled user experience it's
being wasted. In the tech world, software developers see the app experience as defining the company. If a user finds the experience slow, or
complex, or not intuitive, he or she will abandon their search, delete the
app, and have a long-standing negative impression of the company. In
the private sector, it's quite rare these days to find someone not relentlessly working to improve UX.

But not government. For the last hundred years, public officials
have designed systems from the perspective of themselves and their
bureaucracy, not from studying the people who use the services. We
start with UX as a new business proposition for government.

Until recently, suffering from the hangover of highly centralized
legacy systems from the 1970s and 1980s many IT officials viewed their
jobs as processing transactions, maintaining oversight of hardware, and
controlling data. These mainframe programs, developed theoretically to
assist city workers, were usually dictated by compliance requirements
implemented by consultants without either sufficient worker input or
an eye to employee UX.

That has begun to change. The U.K. Digital Service and the U.S.
18F office at the federal General Services Administration serve as consultants to other government agencies, producing early examples of a
citizen-centric orientation. For example, the Digital Service helped the
land registry department reorient its mission from an agency that stores
records to one that makes it easy for property owners to make better
decisions. The range of its services extends to such critical and important areas as teaching bureaucrats how to write clearly. Even the language
it uses to describe its work connotes its user orientation: For example,
at one time its website boasted that it produced fishing licenses "so easy
a child can apply."[3]

For distributed governance, UX is also tied to the idea of a nudge,
discussed in chapter 2, both for the type of information presented to

residents and how it is configured. In a sense, Michael Bloomberg initiated this approach early in his mayoral administration in New York City when he required restaurants to post the calories of items on menus. Rather than ban or regulate food that contributes to public health risks, the calorie counts simply give the consumer more complete information, which will nudge some customers to healthier behaviors.

Louisville uses these approaches, derived from behavioral science, by configuring individuals' "choice architectures"—the social, psychological, and physical contexts in which they make decisions. Starting with a simple pilot, the city redesigned its communications "to encourage residents to pay up, notifying those with unpaid tickets, for instance, that three-quarters of the people in their neighborhood had paid their fines on time in the past year. The new letters more than doubled payments, generating a net return of $4.53 per letter."[4]

The few cities that have nudge units use the concept for a specific goal. However, the idea of the nudge is central to the entire concept of UX. When an event is featured on the city's home page, more individuals will participate in that event. What information a field worker receives on her mobile device—and in what format—affects how she exercises her judgment. None of this is inherently good or bad but, rather, a recognition that sophisticated design guides action, and these two issues cannot be divorced from each other.

Keeping a Close Eye on Pittsburgh

Pittsburgh offers a window into what can emerge when a city puts users front and center. Burgh's Eye View, an app that was launched in late 2016, gives residents insight into a broad range of citywide and neighborhood data, including crime and other public safety incidents, code violations, and 311 service requests, with even more content planned. Developed by the city's analytics team, the app features a simple, catchall search bar and date range that allows users to select the data they want to see on a map of the city and a mobile-optimized layout for use on smartphones. Residents looking to see crime in their neighborhood over the past month, for example, can select the date range, select only the "Police Blotter" layer, and focus on where they live. If they want to consider what parts of the city have amenities they can select pools and recreation areas; if they want to see where problems exist they can select abandoned cars on the street and barking dog summons.

From the start, Burgh's Eye View was focused on what data the user would really want, not just what data the city had available. After an embezzlement scandal rocked the police department in 2014, the newly installed police chief saw data as a concrete way to move the department forward and start a new era. The analytics team, led by Laura Meixell, spent countless hours following officers as they went about their jobs, to understand what combinations of data would be most useful to the department. As Meixell explains of her six team members, all but one of which have public policy degrees, "We are policy curious and never look at our work as a data engineer. We try and ask, 'How would the user want to view the data?' "

In a few months the agency had an impressive data map for the police that included twenty-four law enforcement categories, as well as 311 requests and major capital projects. Rather than assessing one data point at a time, dozens could be correlated and geocoded on a map in real time. The development team focused on reducing barriers that blocked the way to a broader audience. "The way you make data matter for people who aren't data scientists is through visualization, and probably the most successful kind of visualization that exists is a map," says Nick Hall, open data services engineer for Pittsburgh.[5]

As other departments saw what the police had, they wanted in as well, and the team applied the same approach. Once the value of the maps to the public became clear, the group took on the assignment of developing maps for resident groups. Here, too, the user experience was paramount. Even after release, the Burgh's Eye View team presented the app and accepted suggestions in a continuous stream of community meetings. "I think we have been to every community basement and Catholic high school auditorium in the city demonstrating the platform and hearing how to make it better," Meixell says.

The city and Mayor Bill Peduto were committed to widely broadcasting the new site and rolled out a social media campaign and created

YouTube videos to explain to even the most IT-phobic residents how to use the platform. The app even has a mascot, a penguin holding a magnifying glass, and depending on what data the user wants to view in the app, the penguin image changes; when a citizen looks at budget data, the penguin is holding a calculator; or when looking at crime, the penguin is wearing a police cap. The visual, playful, and responsive presentation is a sign to a user that this site isn't just for the civic tech community; it's ready for anyone.

Context Provides Value

As the Burgh's Eye View shows, while it's useful to see crime patterns on your block over time, it can be even more useful if that map also includes building code violations, so you can see if blighted properties are attracting more crime—and use that information to change policing patterns or rally neighbors to advocate for the city to enforce code violations on abandoned properties. Or imagine if you could compare the location of auto accidents with which streets have bicycle lanes and parking restrictions. You might choose a different route to ride home after work, or you might ask your city council representative to install more bicycle lanes.

Actions and data gather value when they are understood in terms of other information, when they have context. That can be spatial (for example, location), subject matter (for example, air quality or building permits), or social (for example, community partnerships or race). User interfaces provide true context when easily understood open data is coupled with helpful tools such as geographic information system (GIS) imagery and enhanced opportunities to collaborate.

Highly visual, configurable data is now easily available for local officials and community leaders to derive UX-informed sites that can offer solutions to hundreds of municipal issues. In Los Angeles for example, a new app from the city, Street Wize, turns data from the planning department into maps that show construction projects happening in each neighborhood, improving coordination across city departments that, in turn, reduces citizen disruptions. Residents can use the app to get greater insight into what's happening on their street, private developers can use it to plan strategically around opportunities to build, and commercial apps like Waze can incorporate information from the database to better inform its users with another layer of real-time data on activity on city streets.

A Lens for Equity

A municipality supports an engaged citizenry when it moves from a self-centered organizational structure to one that places the resident at the center. For example, departments need to contextualize information for residents in a way that provides a shared sense of community. In little ways, then, context can communicate a sense of respect—signage in the city office that can be read by a resident who does not speak English or opportunities for a disabled caller to understand the answers when contacting the city.

Context also matters with respect to bridging the gaps in cities between the wealthy and the poor or between residents of color and those who are white. With better UX, a city can make it easier to discern city response times by community or traffic stops by race. It can prioritize demographic information contrasted to areas in the city that are affected by poverty, blight, absence of jobs, or poor transportation in well-visualized, interactive formats, giving residents and the media information to fully understand patterns in the city and, when applicable, to advocate for change.

The UX framework can also help cities explore how all citizens experience city services and programs, shining a light on possible blind spots. For example, several years ago Seattle mayor Greg Nickels undertook a methodical process that enabled city workers to recognize the impact of agency policy on diverse communities. Seattle created a Racial Equity Toolkit that, essentially, asked city agencies to assess how their work affects minority communities. The kit provided a step-by-step blueprint for how to solicit and then apply input from various departmental program assessments. Seattle understood that no matter what the issue, context matters and can help generate equitable treatment. "It's just a piece of paper with some questions on it, but these are the questions that never get asked," says Elliott Bronstein in the Mayor's Office of Civil Rights.[6]

New Orleans mayor Mitch Landrieu used a decidedly data-centric focus to address inequity in the city. In 2016 he tasked Oliver Wise, his top data analyst, with evaluating a range of service systems to see if there was inequity and, if so, what could be done about it. One of the first areas the city evaluated was emergency response time. Poorer neighborhoods in New Orleans had argued that ambulances take far too long to arrive when called. The data office ran the numbers, and the difference between the 8th district (encompassing the downtown business area and the historic French Quarter) and the 4th district (Algiers, a working-class, predominately African American community) was striking. Seeing the inequity in the numbers alone was not a solution. To learn more, Wise and his team engaged in ride-alongs with ambulance drivers and focused on user-engagement survey work with hospital administrators and vehicle dispatchers. They found that the entire fleet congregated in the 8th district, which is centrally located and which generates most of the emergency calls.

When Wise went back and created a data model to see what would happen if just a few of the ambulance drivers were stationed in more outlying areas, such as the 4th district, he found that spreading a few vehicles out would not compromise efficiency. "You had a situation like a kids' soccer game where all the four-year olds bunch up around the ball. You need to spread out," he says. When the city followed this recommendation, emergency responsiveness improved by 15 percent in the poorer and more far-flung parts of the city and did not drop for anyone else. Wise notes the benefit of using a data strategy by saying, "Considering equity and race is really about assessing outcomes over outputs. Really, you can think of it as user-centric design; we are looking to see how services are received by various communities."

CITIZEN-FOCUSED UX

As noted in chapter 2, more cities are offering open data from city departments, available in a modifiable form, with terms that allow for reuse and redistribution. Open data is a huge step forward for cities, but it, alone, is not sufficient for the move to distributed governance. Cities need to do more than provide a series of complex, comma-delineated datasets that are scattered among different agency websites. The next step is thinking about how the data can be used by a wide number of residents by making it easy to read and understand—and the step after that is promoting it so residents and local organizations know it's available and what it can provide. That's a true test of good UX.

City officials thinking about UX also must understand that today's civic data is generated not just from the standard municipal agency datasets but also from sensors, smartphones, and geocoded photos. According to Peter Hemmersam at the Institute of Urbanism and Landscape, "Ubiquitous computing promises that data handling, sorting, and displaying will no longer be restricted to technical spaces, but disappear into the 'fabric of everyday life' . . . [suggesting a] composite gathering, sharing, and dissemination of real-time data in socially relevant urban contexts."[7]

The city needs to incorporate data that originates from a signal that a stoplight is malfunctioning or from a resident who takes and tags a picture of a problem. To realize the potential of this ocean of information, this data also needs to be curated and presented in a way that is understandable and relevant to disparate users on their terms. One can imagine two years from now, the event organizers at a Pittsburgh community meeting focusing on air quality and noise could by then see IoT sensor information incorporated in the maps—maybe the Burgh's Eye View penguin would, unfortunately, need earplugs by then.

Intermediary Organizations and UX

When it comes to truly effective outreach to the underserved and digitally less involved residents in a city, community intermediaries such as faith-based groups, neighborhood organizations, and social service providers can be particularly useful. These groups can bring better services to their community's residents by showing them how to leverage new platforms, like Burgh Eye's View, as well as how the public data can help them advocate for their neighborhoods. The participation of a trusted nonprofit group also enhances confidence by doubtful neighbors who put their faith in well-visualized data made available by the government but customized by a civic group acting as an intermediary.

Chicago provides a great example of how public officials committed to open data, working with a trusted intermediary, can, together, make data both available and useful to residents. Building on their early successful efforts with WindyGrid, an internal map-based program built to monitor city data, in 2016 Brenna Berman, then the Chicago's CIO, and Chief Data Officer Tom Schenk produced OpenGrid, an open-source geospatial application that provides residents with easy access to city data from multiple devices, including desktop computers, tablets, and phones. OpenGrid brings the data available on the city's portal to life, allowing users to navigate through advanced search functionality or create customizable maps. Chicago envisions OpenGrid serving not only as a resource to residents locally and in other cities, but also as a low-cost business intelligence tool for nonprofits and corporations that wish to take advantage of its capabilities.[8] The city holds weekly open conference calls with developers, who share requests for new features and report bugs.

Key to the success of OpenGrid is the partnership with Smart Chicago Collaborative, a civic organization that focuses on improving residents' lives through technology. Through its Civic User Testing Group, Smart Chicago compensates residents from all corners of the city to test civic websites and apps. These tests not only engage a wide swath of residents in the development process but provide valuable information to developers seeking to enhance their apps' usability and performance. For OpenGrid, citizens tested the platform and provided feedback on its usability to the city.

The intermediaries that power a distributed network come in many forms, and their needs for better city UX vary, as well. Community boards need user interfaces that allow them to easily see and manipulate data about their neighborhoods. Advocacy groups want the ability to use open data to evaluate the city's response to environmental or racial equity issues. Parent groups need information on school bus routes and schedules for library story time. The city cannot tailor its work for every advocacy group, but it can post data in a manner that can be easily seen and managed by a group according to its interests.

Omni-Channel Service

In every sense government should produce the best experience for its residents, regardless of which medium (channel) they might choose to be informed and no matter whether they are simply calling for information or requesting a license. Take, for example, the revitalization that started eight years ago at the chronically underperforming Indiana Bureau of Motor Vehicles (BMV) by Ron Stiver, who came to the job from a marketing and sales position at Eli Lilly's osteoporosis unit, where he led new product efforts. The primary outlet for retail state services—and where many residents form their first impression of how well the state works—the BMV experience offered everything that makes citizens complain about government. It was inconvenient and aggravating, every step was slow, and there was nothing you could do about it.

Stiver launched "Customer Choices," a program that allowed citizens to conduct BMV business through partnerships with 300 automotive dealerships, seven AAA locations, and other nongovernment entities, as well as mobile BMV branches. Moving as many transactions online as possible helped both customers and state employees, so he introduced a $5 discount for online registrations, with a supporting promotional program and the launch of a new myBMV customer portal. Everything changed inside the branches, as well, from the look and feel of the design to the ability to schedule an appointment or monitor wait times online before heading to the facility. Putting the customer first meant abandoning the old model of self-inflicted wounds, where the agency had specific, uniform expiration dates for various licenses, like at the end of a month, creating peaks and valleys in the workflow and unnecessarily long waiting lines.

"We understood that accessing our services was a necessary interruption in Hoosiers' lives. Our simple charge was to minimize that disruption via improved choice and convenience—and to do so without sacrificing quality. By better engaging citizens where they already are, we could improve virtually all aspects of our operating performance," Stiver says.

The results spoke for themselves. Customer satisfaction improved from 70 percent to 97 percent. Average customer visit time at branches decreased from thirty minutes to less than nine. There was a 400 percent increase in registrations processed online, and the average speed-to-answer time at call centers improved from 8.5 minutes to one minute, with abandoned call rates reduced from 32 percent to 5.5 percent. According to Peter Lacy, the current bureau commissioner, online and third-party use now exceeds 50 percent of the BMV transactions.

The Indiana story is not merely one of transformation to better UX. Stiver wanted to give the user as many viable ways as possible to easily discharge their necessary state requirements. When government considers a wide array of options, it is truly considering the full user experience. For example, the opportunity to encourage SMS-based services compared to other public service channels provides options that are "less intrusive than phone calls, cheaper than Internet-based services, and more flexible in time and place as the recipients can read the messages at their leisure and choose when to respond."[9]

Retailers call this approach omni-channel marketing, and Stiver's early use of it in Indiana sets a precedent for the new O/S. A city or state government organizing itself around its citizens will offer multiple channels combined with a strategy to encourage customers to migrate to the channel they find easiest to use and most efficient. One person might not care about how pleasant it is now in the government vehicle office— she would much rather replace a lost driver's license online. Another "customer" however might want to talk to someone face-to-face when getting a learner's permit, and he might appreciate that new paint and better customer service training for staff at the BMV.

Personalized UX

The ultimate in a citizen-centered experience would be a personalized page—the Amazoning of government. For example, the Danish Citizen Portal (borger.dk) uses a digital signature and user-design techniques to offer a secure "My Page" section, where a citizen can access data specifically targeted to himself or herself about the economy, housing, property values, or financial obligations to the government. My Page consolidates relevant services into a single personalized space.[10]

In the United States, few have thought more about how local government interacts with residents than Joe Morrisroe, the long-time, extraordinarily competent director of the high-volume NYC311 call center. Morrisroe and his team handle more than 36 million contacts per year. In 2003, he helped Mayor Bloomberg build the then best-in-class centralized call center, allowing any New Yorker to call about almost anything and get an answer—at the time a highly futuristic idea. In 2006 his team added online, text, and mobile options.

Technology moves quickly, though, and a call center strictly focused on the telephone has become outdated. So Morrisroe has taken on one of the nation's most ambitious efforts to transform service delivery and customer engagement. His goal is to build a Customer Relationship Management (CRM) platform that incorporates a seamless omni-channel experience for customers and service providers, personalized accounts for residents, enhanced open data capabilities, and integration with IoT. As a result, NYC311 will provide more customer choice and convenience, moving from answering questions and complaints to a model of individual accounts that preemptively provides customized information even before the question is asked.

The new system will consolidate resident information into one portal—a window into the city, not just an easier way for residents to complain. Its UX incorporates a broad array of information that artificial intelligence (AI) translates into personalized communications, including data from IoT sensors; city documents; permits and plans; reliable third-party information like Waze; and other sources. To reach this level of coordination and personalization, Morrisroe plans to allow residents to opt in to NYC311 and then organize the data for them.

Public school parents will be able to get registration dates and enrollment requirements, discover after-school programs, and track school or class progress. Residents will be able to consolidate and track payments for water billing, property taxes, and more, and use maps to review health, crime, cleanliness, and resiliency data at neighborhood and block levels. Small business owners will have the ability to automate water meter readings, renew licenses, and pay for violations.

"This is our opportunity to expand the dynamic between the customer and government and make city life a little easier for New Yorkers by allowing them to access, store, and utilize city information and data on their terms and for their needs," Morrisroe says. "The new platform puts information in the hands of the customer."

Even as NYC311 sets new standards for city responsiveness, the frontier continues to move. Cities need to understand that when they are designing around a citizen today, that resident is as likely to ask Siri a question as to search for the answer on her browser. Call centers powered by cognitive learning and natural language will enable virtual assistants to address a wide variety of questions in real time as the machines read current social media and city documents. Given the recent private-sector advances with virtual assistants like Siri, Alexa, and Cortana, the use of artificially intelligent assistants should be part of the operating system, particularly for the next 311 generation.[11]

Los Angeles recently began using a cloud-based virtual assistant named Chip in its Business Assistance Virtual Network. Chip answers questions related to opportunities to do business with the city, such as searching for contract opportunities or identifying the correct business classification code. The chatbot "learns" and adds additional answers over time based on interactions with users; it has already cut emails to the department by more than half.[12] These tools may not be for all residents, but they can be part of an ecosystem that matches channels and information with the preferences of the customer while freeing up public employee time to work on complex problems.

UX Driving Citizen Participation

Secrecy builds distrust even when information is technically available to the public but too opaque to be useful. Citizen-centered design creates value by making it easier to understand the actions, goals, and efforts of City Hall. It also can enhance civic capacity and spur civic action, which brings us back to the Dewey principle of leadership, calling together the public in a way that fuels its capacity of expressing its wants and needs as a community. Community boards now use Burgh's Eye View crime data to better focus local organizing efforts and help improve how the community interfaces with local law enforcement. Burgh's Eye View works because its contextualized, well-visualized data on critical issues can bring together a public informed by facts.

Cities can also explicitly use UX to gather information from residents and organizations and to encourage their participation in civic issues. Stories in the *LA Times* about how poorer parts of the city were receiving inferior trash service sparked the city to map cleanliness ratings that help communities advocate for better practices and assist city leaders in monitoring results.

In this sense leadership has two challenges, both of which require community respect and confidence. The first involves the ability to call the community together in support of a bold goal—a new transit line or a large investment that would spur a new approach to economic development. The second relates to the less visible goals of operational excellence extolled in this book. The public does not pay close attention to the manner in which government is manufactured and, therefore, the status quo, even if mediocre, can be maintained by a small focused group that benefits from it in the absence of a clamor for change. The public leader needs to create a climate for informed action by using well-visualized data to support a narrative that demands more for his or her community—an intolerance for the mediocre and an appetite for results. This public support for change will provide courage and support for those public employees who strive for better outcomes.

Note that community is not always neatly defined by geographic boundaries any more than it is by the relatively artificial boundaries associated with a municipality. Andrea di Maio, an analyst with the information technology consulting firm Gartner, writes:

> People on social media are aggregating and re-arranging in new and unpredictable ways, cutting across organizational and geographical boundaries, forming and dissolving bonds, coalescing around a cause to then scatter separately in different directions . . . Rules of residence, immigration, citizenship apply to processes that take from days to years to be completed. But in social media I can join a platform, a group, a cause today and leave tomorrow.[13]

Cities may need to be creative to educate communities to build citizen participation. In the totally interconnected city, objects designed for one purpose can have multiple functions. As Andrew Vande Moere and Dan Hill point out, using kiosks as an example:

> Because of its unique qualities, urban visualization has the theoretical ability to persuade . . . Through sensing technology, a display can act as a tool that increases the capability to capture a behavior (e.g., measuring residential energy consumption, bicycle use, etc.); through its visual imagery, it can function as a medium that provides useful information, such as behavioral statistics or cause-and-effect relationships; and through its networking ability, it can become a social actor, encouraging community-based feedback and social interaction.[14]

Active outreach can also include ideas like online games or augmented reality that allow residents to see a new park or the effects of a zoning change. Gamification is essentially one type of nudge—an initiative informed by psychology that changes the context in which people make decisions to influence their behavior. Salem, Massachusetts, launched a game called "What's The Point" to encourage local participation in neighborhood revitalization plans. Developed by Emerson College's Engagement Game Lab, the program sought resident ideas for neighborhood improvements and rewarded posts with virtual coins. Users could pledge these coins toward causes in their community, and the top three causes won real money.[15]

In 2016 Los Angeles began to experience an affordable housing crisis where residents in rent-controlled units faced illegal evictions so that some landlords could illegally convert units to market rate. The city turned to its Innovation Team (i-team) with its capacity to take on special projects in nontraditional ways. By putting the user front and center in a careful design process, i-team director Amanda Daflos approached the project in a method more typical of the new O/S than standard city government.

Under the guidance of design strategy lead Bora Shin, whose career included working in social enterprises designing products for nonprofits, data scientist Alex Pudlin, and project manager Jason Neville, whose career included working in planning and housing issues, the team combined its data analytics, project management, communication, and design skills to approach the problem in a more creative manner. The preparation and the campaign itself ultimately involved real stories of tenants who eventually stood with Los Angeles mayor Eric Garcetti when the city launched the storytelling piece of the campaign.

To start, Daflos brought in Palo Alto-based design firm IDEO to conduct a half-day workshop around residential displacement with staff from housing that involved prototyping. The team gathered input from tenant and landlord organizations at workshops in English and Spanish to learn more about the situation, including what vulnerable communities might most want to know. They curated data like the location of rent stabilized units around the city to understand who to interview to develop their campaign and where to target for outreach to get the most from their limited budget.

"The data and discussions also helped us determine the best methods for outreach, based on how participants receive information. We gathered with the renters and presented several drafts and they identified which type would be most valuable for them," Daflos says. "We learned so much through these workshops including [that] communities see home as more than just a living space, it extends to their neighbors and their neighborhood. They associate home with the entire community."

The human-centered design process in L.A. followed an established path, one infrequently used by government, that includes choosing the group to be served, exploring the problem and workable solutions with them, developing a prototype intervention, and then testing and iterating it.[16] The design sensitivity in the development of the L.A. campaign had an effect almost immediately. Focusing on residents most likely to be displaced by landlords trying to avoid rent control caps to, in turn, deter those landlords, the city designed outreach efforts and tools that operated much more effectively than traditional whack-a-mole enforcement efforts. Within two months of the launch, the website had been visited nearly 10,000 times, 4,400 pocket guides were downloaded, and call volumes to the city's housing call center rose significantly.

UX FOR PUBLIC EMPLOYEES

Each day public employees are face-to-face with residents who are asking for service, applying for a permit, sitting in a classroom, injured or sick, victims of a crime, or in any number of other situations. The O/S emphasizes worker discretion—the capacity of public servants to see new opportunities to do their jobs better. With this increased autonomy, how well the civil servant does his or her job is dependent, in large part, on rapid synthesis of information and observations.

When a hotel clerk can see a frequent customer's complete record when she checks in, he can see if she complained last time about noise, and he has the authority to adjust, on the spot, her assigned room to one away from the street. With instantly available, easy-to-use information and permission not to follow immaterial rules, he can produce satisfaction. Contrast this to the highly publicized event where a United Airlines employee faced with an overbooked flight followed the rules that instructed him to call in a Chicago Airport Police Officer, who followed the rule to forcibly remove a passenger. Those employees did not need any information about the passenger they evicted, or any suggestions on alternative solutions, because they had no discretion.

In Allegheny County, in Pennsylvania, as we discuss in chapter 5, frontline child welfare workers now receive welfare, school, criminal justice, and school transfer information about the child and family while they are onsite. That chapter discusses what it takes to gather and organize the information, but to be effective that data needs to be curated and presented in a way that allows the worker to understand and use it in the field.

The conversion from paper to digital processes enables efficient delivery of information, and a shift to municipal IT systems designed to help the public employee solve problems will power better outcomes and higher citizen satisfaction. To design with employees in mind, government officials can start by identifying the most significant areas where their workers could make more discerning and quicker judgments if they had better and easier access to important data. The design team should identify the specific job assigned to the employee, identify all the sources of data that will enhance her discretion and her ability to do her job well, and then present it in a fashion to further those results. The design process for employee and resident UX are similar in that the orientation of the designer is tightly focused on the specific user. Often an initiative around one group leads to a success for others, too, as was the case with Burgh's Eye View.

When a city is thinking about how to use UX in its materials for employees, the team should consider how to use nudges based on be- havioral science, just as they do for citizens. How field workers receive information drives their behavior, too. A maintenance worker who can see not only the street that requires a pavement repair but also the drain- age problem under it will more likely look for underlying causes than one who doesn't.

The NYPD Domain Awareness System (DAS) was jump started when Police Commissioner Bill Bratton returned to New York City for his second tour of duty under newly elected mayor Bill de Blasio, and the effort has continued under current commissioner James O'Neill. Both commissioners provided field officers with more freedom and au- thority to make decisions. To support that mandate, the NYPD had to develop new technology that enabled this change.

The NYPD had a well-earned reputation for professionalism and use of sophisticated management and analytic techniques. The depart- ment also did not lack for information: readings flow in from 911 calls, license plate readers, closed-circuit cameras, environmental sensors, and police documents like case reports and warrants. Yet the complexity and size of the NYPD meant that data analysis was typically done at head- quarters, where specially trained employees evaluated information. To realize Bratton and O'Neill's vision, that had to change.

To help a cop charged with making instantaneous, challenging deci- sions, the NYPD's DAS takes literally billions of records and translates them into useful information, both as dispatches formatted for an easy- to-use interface on a smartphone and as alerts on a desktop application. Officers can be alerted when a wanted car is scanned by a license plate reader, or when gunshots are reported near a high-profile location.

In the last few years, under the direction of Deputy Commissioner of Information Technology Jessica Tisch, advanced analytics have been built into the DAS. For example, in the past, to detect patterns of crime, such as burglaries, detectives and officers had to remember prior crimes that were similar. Crime analysts typically focused on detecting patterns within their precincts, but criminals don't care about precinct boundaries. Now, a new "Patternizr" module built into DAS uses machine learning algorithms on crime data to help analysts detect patterns with less manual effort.

Patternizr essentially gives a crime analyst a ranked list of the most similar crimes, almost like a Netflix recommendation algorithm. Patternizr was trained on historical NYPD patterns, meaning it learned from the collective institutional knowledge of the city's crime analysts. The algorithm ingests structured and unstructured fields from crime reports, such as the time and place of occurrence, the method of entry, and whether force was used. It also parses the narratives, looking for keywords that stand out. Because the algorithm can look through many crimes quickly, it isn't limited by precinct boundaries and can more easily identify similar crimes that happened years ago.

DAS succeeds because NYPD had its officers involved with the technical team in each step of the development. This led to software that better matched the officers' needs, but the partnership also generated support in the department because it led to officers feeling ownership of the end product. In addition, the openness of the process meant street cops and detectives understood what made the system tick; rather than being presented with a mysterious black box, they understood its logic because many were part of the open process to create it.

CompStat, the NYPD initiative that connects crime data to police performance, also underwent a change driven by this new approach to democratize as much information as possible. The original Comp-Stat—a weekly meeting where senior police officials asked precinct commanders detailed questions about crime and operations in their jurisdictions—relied on a book of statistics distributed to commanders prior to the meeting. At the end of the Bloomberg administration, the NYPD added an interactive software module called CompStat 2.0 into DAS that allows officers to visualize and interact with the data.[17] Designed with the commanders and their analysts in mind, the easily used visualization software enhances the officers' understanding and makes the CompStat meeting a more productive and collaborative event.

A NEVER-ENDING EFFORT

As cities consider and then launch programs similar to NYPD Domain Awareness System for their frontline-level crime fighters (and analogous programs for maintenance workers, social workers, and building inspectors), they will need to transparently address questions concerning privacy and surveillance. To the extent these efforts also involve shared data, controlled access should also be addressed, as well. For example, should truancy information be broadly or narrowly shared between a school social worker and the neighborhood cop? Data sharing and domain aware access will produce better decisions, but the benefits will exceed the costs only if carefully set up and monitored.

For citizen-focused UX, too, personalization and citizen-relation management raise important privacy and security issues that will be driven by a municipality's policies and practices. Is the CRM an opt-in only process? How much data will be needed to connect two separate events to the same individual—phone number, name, address?—and how does one connect a mobile phone to a physical address? When well designed, this connection can significantly aid the resident's interaction. Nevertheless, cities will need policies concerning when a broad CRM should allow an official to deny a resident a city privilege, contract, or license when he owes taxes or fines to the city, for example. How much nexus is needed to deprive a business operating as a limited liability corporation of a license because of the acts of an officer or owner? Will strictness increase as the importance of its application increases? It may be one thing to temporarily deny a building permit until the applicant can show the error of an identification verification match but quite a different matter if the issue is an arrest.

Even as these concerns are considered and a widespread UX mindset becomes the norm in city government, this effort to improve the user experience will never stop, requiring constant measurement of both citizen satisfaction and utilization patterns. Feedback can be gathered from outbound voice surveys, requests for SMS texts back about a service ("How was your experience today at the Bureau of Motor Vehicles?"), or an app that asks for details on the timeliness and quality of the experience—from the time the citizen requested the pothole be filled until the work was completed.

Cities also should build processes into their IT systems that monitor how well their UX is working. Retailers study where and when a customer leaves the website. They track when he or she gets to the shopping cart but fails to complete the online purchase. Cities need to look at abandonment rates—where they are losing residents who could finish a transaction, such as registering for a permit, but don't. Which site designs assure residents and encourage them to spend time on the site until they solve their problem? More and more cities and states, using the behavioral economics approach, are already monitoring their UX with A/B testing to determine whether one communication design affects behaviors differently than another. This testing includes such diverse areas as showing up for prenatal care, a job interview, or a probation appointment, through a well-worded text. These comparisons raise ethical issues, but a design that fails to consider the implication of the nudge will miss important value.

UX is the first topic in this book's deeper exploration of the building blocks of a new O/S not only because it represents a key concept of a distributed system but because its centrality will keep government focused on what counts: serving and partnering with the public to develop local satisfaction, pride, and trust. Governments that truly wish to enhance resident trust will never cease analyzing citizen satisfaction in terms of their experience and service. Fundamental to the new O/S, the user design will show citizens that their government is designed around service to them.

Chapter 3 **THE BOTTOM LINE**

Key Points

- A full commitment to the user experience is central to the new operating system. In the business world, UX is about being sure the customer gets the most from the product; the same principle needs to be applied to government.

▪ UX demands an incessant focus on making the information and services citizens receive as easy to understand and navigate as possible.

▪ Every time a citizen interacts with government it builds or erodes trust; UX is critical to winning that trust back.

▪ UX can and should be considered for city employees, as well as for citizens. Good UX makes civil servants more effective by helping them solve problems with the assistance of well visualized, easy to understand data.

Pitfalls

▪ Cities can't depend only on website updates and 311 systems. UX requires government to consider that citizens prefer information and services across many channels.

▪ City Hall must demonstrate the seriousness with which it takes data privacy and security by establishing clear and transparent policies and a process to ensure those policies are followed.

Recommendations

▪ Most policy implementation begins with an internal focus by the administering agency. Instead, the very first step must be design thinking around the user.

▪ Context is critical to good UX and comes in many varieties, including spatial and demographic. Aim to include as many contexts as possible, and a system for updating them.

▪ UX must be applied to multiple channels, including SMS text, mobile, email, and in-person communication.

▪ A sure sign of good UX is citizen engagement. Rather than just being pleased with service, government communication should engender citizen participation in service and policy reforms.

Examples

▪ With Burgh's Eye View, the city of Pittsburgh has created an easily navigable map that allows citizens and community groups to plug in hundreds of different data points to better understand crime, neighborhood development, and health.

▪ New Orleans adds context to its data, including how race affects certain policies, to arrive at a more equitable distribution.

▪ The New York City Police Department's Domain Awareness System harnesses massive amounts of data from diverse sources to discern patterns in crime and generates highly contextualized information for the street officer.

NOTES

1. Edelman, "Trust and the U.S. Presidential Election" (www.edelman .com/trust2017/trust-and-us-presidential-election).

2. Geoff Mulgan, *The Art of Public Strategy: Mobilizing Power and Knowledge for the Common Good* (Oxford University Press, 2009), p. 2.

3. See U.K. Government: Government Digital Service, "Angling to Meet User Needs at Defra" (https://gds.blog.gov.uk/2017/03/21/angling-to-meet-user -needs-at-defra).

4. Stephen Goldsmith, "How Government Can Nurture the Nudge," *Governing*, May 2017 (www.governing.com/blogs/bfc/col-louisville-nudge-behaviorally -informed-intervention.html).

5. Robert Burack, "Burgh's Eye View: How Pittsburgh Built an Agile Product Shop," *Data-Smart City Solutions*, December 2016 (http://datasmart .ash.harvard.edu/news/article/burghs-eye-view-951).

6. Neil Kleiman and Tom Hillard, "Innovation and the City," *Center for an Urban Future and NYU Wagner* (November 2016).

7. Peter Hemmersam and others, "Exploring Urban Data Visualization and Public Participation in Planning," *Journal of Urban Technology* 22 (April 2016), p. 47.

8. Sean Thornton, "Civic App Replication Goes to Market," *Data-Smart City Solutions*, May 2016 (http://datasmart.ash.harvard.edu/news/article /opengrid-for-smart-cities-842).

9. Tony Dwi Susanto and Robert Goodwin, "User Acceptance of SMS-Based E-Government Services," *Government Information Quarterly* 30 (August 2013), p. 491.

10. John Bertot, Elsa Estevez, and Tomasz Janowski, "Universal and Contextualized Public Services: Digital Public Service Innovation Framework," *Government Information Quarterly* 33 (April 2016), pp. 211–22.

11. Stephen Goldsmith, "Artificial Intelligence Will Help Create a More Responsive Government," *Government Technology*, February 2017 (www.gov tech.com/opinion/Artificial-Intelligence-Will-Help-Create-a-More-Responsive -Government.html).

12. Theo Douglas, "Los Angeles, Microsoft Unveil Chip: New Chatbot Project Centered on Streamlining," *Government Technology*, May 3, 2017 (www.gov tech.com/computing/Los-Angeles-Microsoft-Unveil-Chip-New-Chatbot -Project-Centered-on-Streamlining.html).

13. Andrea di Maio, "Welcome to the United States of Facebook," *Gartner*, February 7, 2011 (http://blogs.gartner.com/andrea_dimaio/2011/02/07/welcome -to-the-united-states-of-facebook).

14. Andrew Vande Moere and Dan Hill, "Designing for the Situated and Public Visualization of Urban Data," *Journal of Urban Technology* 19, no. 2 (April 2012), pp. 25–46.

15. Stephen Goldsmith, "Gamifying Government," *Government Technology* (September 2017).

16. Michael Mintrom, "Design Thinking in Policymaking Processes: Opportunities and Challenges," *Australian Journal of Public Administration* 75 (September 2016).

17. E. S. Levine and others, "The NYPD Department's Domain Awareness System," *INFORMS* 47 (January 2017), pp. 1–15.

FOUR

Government That Acts in Time

Bill is a small homebuilder who uses essentially the same set of blue-prints for every house he constructs. He has a family who must be in their new home within six months or they will need to rent a place until the house is finished. Bill faces long waits for city permits to get started on the project.

With a part-time job and two young children, Denise gets by, but it's a struggle. She qualifies for several city programs to help with expenses like child care, but to apply, she needs to take time off from work, and is often asked to produce the same documents and information for one program that she's already provided in another city office for another benefit.

Mary raised money from friends and family to open her first restaurant. Margins will be thin, but she picked a good location and understands the market, so she has confidence she can make it work. Now she's paying rent every month, and it's eating away at her capital because she can't open until the city finishes the last of its multiple approvals and inspections.

Every time there's a heavy rain, Joe's basement fills with water because the city's storm sewers overflow and back up. He called the city engineering department with an idea about constructing a pond to collect the water, but the department says they have no program in place to do planning with the community—but the maintenance department will respond after the flooding occurs.

Charlene is a city inspector in the Planning Department, almost done with a permit for a residential garage. She's done except for a final okay on her form from Transportation, but that department has a backlog and Charlene's paperwork request is a low priority. Until she gets that routine signoff, though, the homeowner will have to wait.

In *Poor Richard's Almanack*, Benjamin Franklin wrote, "Lost time is never found again."[1] Every single day across every city in America, old operating systems slow down administrators' ability to do their jobs, which in ways big and small cause citizens to lose time. The wealthy can hire lawyers and expediters for some tasks but that delivers an equally troubling message of unfairness and arrogance, particularly when many government programs designed to support low-income households are mired in multiple, complex, time-consuming processes. All these delays and roadblocks cost cities in terms of wealth invested and taxes paid—and the friction built into the system erodes trust in government.

The new O/S can power government to act in time. We borrow the phrase "act in time" from David Ellwood, formerly Dean of Harvard Kennedy School, who applied it in a related but different context, positing that damage from disasters like Hurricane Katrina can be avoided or mitigated if government uses its will and resources to address known issues before trouble strikes. Here we argue that government must understand the relatively minor but real disasters of the cost to itself and its citizens from routine delays. With a new O/S driven by technological breakthroughs, the city can expel needless time delays out of every function of government, from how quickly it takes an official to decide on a money-saving idea to providing services to a family in need.

Regulatory reform is a prime example of the power of acting in time. This chapter explores how a distributed system enables government to identify risks sooner and protect health and safety in newer and more efficient ways that incorporate community feedback while dramatically reducing the time and cost of any relevant compliance.

A new O/S, both the technology and the rules around it, compresses time by providing tools to make ever-greater amounts of information more easily and readily available. We see it every day outside of government. For example a recent article in *Information Week* about "speed to insight" discusses a breakthrough by health insurer Anthem/Well-Point, which was facing a lag of as long as seventy-two hours to respond to a doctor's urgent request for coverage of a treatment. According to author Shanker Ramamurthy:

> The company implemented a system that quickly correlates clinical research, patient data, and clinical practice guidelines to expedite the pre-approval process on doctors' requests. The new system generates hypotheses and uses evidence-based learning to score recommendations on a confidence scale so nurses are given the best options for each patient in a matter of seconds, not hours or days. By shortening the approval time for treatments, WellPoint is reducing costs, improving service, and, most importantly, singling out the most appropriate treatment for each patient.[2]

In a 2016 article on *How to Make Your Company Machine Learning Ready,* author James Hodson wrote, "Over the next five to ten years, the biggest business gains will likely stem from getting the right information to the right people at the right time. Building upon the business intelligence revolution of the past years, machine learning will turbo-charge finding patterns and automate value extraction in many areas."[3]

It's time for government to commit to the same intelligence revolution that has already taken root in the business world, even while recognizing the unique challenges, conditions, and opportunities that affect the public sector. For cities, the AI and machine-learning tools incorporated in a new O/S can mine and organize high quality, highly relevant data and disseminate it more quickly to speed decisions about everything from permit applications to fixing broken streetlights.

OPERATING IN TIME

There is no one reason government actions typically are slow; each situation can have its own bottleneck. Part of the job of getting City Hall to operate quicker is to identify exactly why a task can be so slow and exactly what tools can be brought to bear toward improvement.

In 2010 New Orleans faced an inventory of more than 40,000 abandoned dwellings. Some were dangerous places for children to play and others were eyesores that stood in the way of new development. The New Orleans' Department of Code Enforcement, responsible for tearing down these blighted structures, required its director to make a decision on whether to demolish or sell each blighted property—and the waiting list for her ruling was more than 1,500 properties long. The choice was based on consideration of complex factors, including location, historical significance, market interest, and condition, and the director was the only one with the needed expertise to make those decisions.

In 2014 that began to change. The Department of Code Enforcement asked the city's Office of Performance and Accountability to help with a data-driven solution. The team worked with Code Enforcement staff to understand decision factors, create test cases with different scenarios and the director's final decision, and develop a machine-learning algorithm based on that data. Their solution, a new Blight Scorecard, allows mid-level supervisors to score properties and then receive weighted recommendations about what the decision should be. Because many staff members could use the system's decision-support tool, the department was able to eliminate the director's backlog while also removing all paper components of the process.[4] "With the blight scorecard, our decisions about the fates of blighted properties have become more rigorous, faster, and consistent. With fewer cases in blight purgatory, more [vacant and abandoned] properties are being redeveloped, demolished, or otherwise brought back into compliance," says Oliver Wise, the director of the city's Office of Performance and Accountability.

For a generation or more, bureaucracy has been a bad word. Few and far between are the government employees who introduce themselves at a party as bureaucrats, unless they are aiming for irony. But

TABLE 4-1 *Steps That Speed Action*

OLD SYSTEMS	NEW O/S
Task based; reactive and production-line uniformity	Resources redirected to problems; predictive, targeted interventions
Supervisory approvals required	Less permission, more after-action evaluation of results; fewer layers
Multiple handoffs of files in sequential order	Concurrent digital processes
Designed for paper	Prohibiting paper
A high percentage of routine actions	Routine handled by machine learning and automation; employee time redeployed for complex issues
Time elapsed is not a metric	Cities measure waiting time and associated cost
Work concentrated in agencies	Open, well-visualized data allows staff easy access across agencies

traditional bureaucracy in an older, analog system served a function—increasingly large staffs needed an efficient way to move questions and information written on paper up and then back down the chain of command. Before the digital revolution, government needed a clear, meritocratic, and compliance-based system to fight off corruption and support urban growth. More than a century ago, it was a professional breakthrough when cities prioritized work orders based on when the city received a request for service rather than by the political connections of who made the request.

In a world where well-curated information can be available immediately, much of the rationale, time, and cost of these procedures can go away. An entirely new digital O/S simplifies, speeds, and improves the bureaucratic function while reorganizing the work. With a mixture of the approaches outlined in table 4-1, and discussed in more detail in this section, the commodity work and the routine will be performed by machines, and the bureaucrat will, once again, become a public service worker.

Routines that benefit the day-to-day functions of government can become the enemy in the face of a disruptive event. A highly routinized organization may be cost-efficient but, for that very reason, also be incapable of responding quickly to a sudden and unexpected change in the environment. In these circumstances, an agile system with rapid-cycle processes can respond in time and, in turn, produce dramatic benefit. Faced with a massive storm, for instance, a city's maintenance department equipped with the data and experience to make decisions quickly will be able to help remove downed trees, repair roadways, and assist homeowners much more quickly than a department dependent on work orders and a command-and-control structure.

Even in the most basic ways IT changes now enable municipal organization to operate faster. Any street-level municipal employee with a smartphone, such as an iPhone, has in her pocket a device that is tens of thousands of times more powerful than the computer that guided the Apollo mission to the moon, and 100,000 times faster.[5] Thirty years ago, individuals came to City Hall and provided information, which officials used to fill in forms. Then much of that work was transferred to the applicant by allowing/forcing him to fill in the same multiple forms but now online. These callous processing delays provoked the next wave of still-developing breakthroughs, involving concurrent work where all agencies have access to the same documents (think Google Docs or Dropbox for permitting). These changes make tasks move more quickly, not because less work is being accomplished but because the routine, mechanical work in the old operating system gets redirected to machines, and motivated public service workers with enhanced training and knowledge will now be targeted at the difficult problems or people.

Yet today the city worker still labors making endless calculations and filling in forms. Machine learning could assist. For example, government could take a page from Airbnb, which in its processing noticed that after owners who wanted to rent their space filled in all the routine details, like room sizes and rules about pets and location, they became stuck on pricing, which required more calculations, time, and judgment than the owner could quickly produce.[6] So Airbnb designed a machine response that compared the information the owner had given with vast amounts of relevant information from similar sites and instantly nominated options.

This kind of combination of data and analytics can be applied in many ways.

Speed from analysis: By using newly-available analytic techniques, cities can better identify targets for attention and preemptive interventions in infrastructure, public health, public safety, and more. Municipal governments will be able to broadly identify outliers, such as a certain type of shop owner who pays much less in taxes than similar businesses. Identifying anomalies and correlations speeds up processes by focusing effort where it counts. Based on weather, maintenance data, traffic patterns, and many other variables, a road crew, for example, can identify locations where in time repairs can solve problems before they deteriorate to the point that an accident occurs—and at much less cost.

Speed from sensor tips: Cities could use IoT sensors to identify a water pipe in need of preventative maintenance, accelerating a response. Smart trash bins will tell officials when they need to be emptied, and sophisticated GPS logistics systems will organize the most efficient snowplow routes. Replacing the routine with service that is better informed will address problems more quickly and make the routine more efficient.

Speed from bot answers: Chatbots, using cognitive learning and natural language tools, will answer many routine questions at 311 call centers more quickly and efficiently than their human counterparts. The AI program used by Airbnb or a call center, which reads tens of thousands of documents to acquire vast amounts of knowledge on the issues, could provide decision support services to employees in the field who are struggling with complex questions, speeding their ability to repair a boiler in a government facility or assist a family in need.

Speed from delegating routine to machines: Machines will continue to take over the clerical and administrative tasks that waste hours and hours of every workweek: filling in missing information on forms, finding the applicable case file, filing report notes in standard format. They also will read those same forms to assist employees in identifying patterns—whether of people in need of services or of those individuals most frequently involved in waste, fraud, and abuse—freeing up employees to concentrate on processing these problem cases more quickly.

Speed from concurrent work: Current city operations generally do not support cross-agency coordinated work, do not easily facilitate virtual teams forming up around a problem, and are set up mechanistically to assign tasks, not to solve problems. With a new O/S, as explored in chapter 5, these types of activities can become standard at City Hall, creating new opportunities for innovative programs that can save time and effort.

Speed through fewer permission levels: By delegating discretion downward and removing layers of government, decisions can be made more quickly, with less cost and time delay. By looking at another agency's open data, a city worker can much more quickly find relevant information, obviating the need for a trip to that department and a request for information that usually takes time to produce and process. In both cases—looking for approval up through the chain or working on a matter across multiple agencies—the absence of paper eliminates the wasted time associated with searching for and passing folders.

Speed from eliminating forms: Design thinking will move city regulation away from the concept of forms altogether. As Evan Absher of the Kaufmann Foundation points out, "forms are simply the human readable way of gathering structured data." In this model, the city asks the applicant for some information, augments it with available data, makes that available to various applicable agencies that add to, verify, or discredit the information, and then makes a decision. Andrew Maier lays out a path that a new O/S could follow to design a government with far fewer forms. He breaks form design down into protocol, process, and platform, each of which is currently forged by the use of paper but can be modified for a digital, distributed information system.[7] Regulation according to this process involves gathering and handling data in certain ways to arrive at a level of confidence concerning the proposed commercial activity. The data will be augmented and interrogated depending on the purpose—more focused on the result needed and less on the form required.

To be clear, this new acting in time era is not just a product of the new hardware and software but also of new structures and systems to replace assembly lines with problem-solving. The nature of work itself in city departments will and needs to change through the mix of technical tools and by new procedures and culture. For example, to align with the familiar yet true saw that you measure what you value and value what you measure, cities should begin to keep track of waiting time for tasks. How long from first contacting City Hall until an applicant hears if he or she qualifies for benefits? How long from the approval to install new playground equipment to when children are playing on the site? Government can also score the costs it incurs from delays—lost new revenues or the value of reduced costs.

In the same vein, employees with more tools and authority need better training. Cities will need to ensure civil servants are prepared to work more quickly with new tools and new procedures. As we address in chapter 5, supervisors (whose own job description no longer will include preapproval for manifold tasks by their staffs) will use data insights and dashboards to manage the employees who work for them, as well as how their workers perform in terms of results and fairness. The field- or retail-level worker needs to know how to access and use information that is quickly accessible and organized across agencies.

REGULATING IN TIME

Local and state regulation covers large sectors of the economy, from beauticians and doctors to kitchen repair construction companies and taxi drivers. Economists and politicians debate the role of government regulation with respect to the free market, including how private property rights and pricing can solve problems. This chapter, however, addresses regulation from a less philosophical and more practical perspective, exploring how a new operating system with more transparency and public participation can increase the speed of regulatory structures, enhance health and safety of protections, and impose fewer expenses on would-be licensees and their customers.

Health and safety protection in a local community takes many forms. Insurance companies impose rules on their customers to keep down their costs from claims, like making sure fleet vehicles meet certain standards. Tort lawyers suing for harm to an individual essentially add a cost to unsafe acts, making other individuals and organizations consider how they can avoid incurring that expense. Cities and states pass laws or regulations that set standards, from acquiring a liquor license to building a new supermarket to simply putting up a backyard fence. In some circumstances the government requires a permit; in others it sends inspectors.

Of course regulation does not always work as well as hoped. Given a metric of workplace safety but without any corresponding metric in terms of the cost of time, regulators will tend to slow approval times to try to insure they don't make any decision that can have any negative effect. Certainly safety must be understood in terms of likelihood of harm and in the context of other tradeoffs. Currently there is no real measurement or standard for how much time a permitting process should take.

There are other issues with how cities currently handle regulation, as well. Entrenched interest groups often hijack the regulatory process to protect their interests. Taxi medallions are a classic example. Most cities limit taxi permits (medallions), ostensibly to ensure that only safe vehicles roam the streets. The logic doesn't make much sense on the face of it, since the city could have simply created a set of required safety and consumer protections to operate a taxi and had police enforce those laws. The medallion system makes more sense when it's viewed as a tool to limit competition for current taxi owners.

Sometimes if the cost of compliance with a regulation is set too high, in terms of time and money, it serves as an incentive for noncompliance. A small-time construction worker who does inexpensive kitchen remodeling can be in and out of a job before he receives a permit or before he is caught by an inspector. A system where it is less costly to ignore than follow the rules undermines its very health and safety goals.

To reimagine the city and state regulatory regimes, a new O/S presents several points for intervention.

1. **The risk or policy evaluation phase:** Before regulating at all, government should determine if the activity or industry needs oversight and why.

2. **The origination phase:** If there is sufficient reason to warrant government oversight, the next issue becomes identifying the best method of regulation. Should a license or permit be required, or does disclosure or a law setting a standard or outlawing a practice suffice?

3. **The implementation phase:** If a permit is required, how will the regulated actor obtain it, and in what ways can that process be made simpler and faster? What is the most efficient inspection and enforcement regimen that will accomplish the goals with the least amount of disruption to reputable businesses?[8]

The remaining sections of this chapter explore new options that touch in many ways on all three of these phases, using a data-driven O/S to create new processes that both dramatically shorten time and enhance protections.

In Atlanta, a Faster Permit

Atlanta knows a city can make permitting easier and faster because they made it happen—in just one year. The permitting system in the city's Office of Buildings had operated at a typical speed of government permit approval in cities across the country: a slow slog for homeowners, developers, and small businesses alike. Anyone who needed permits went through a byzantine process with no clear timetable; once a request went in, no one knew when it would come out.

Atlanta took on its successful reform effort after frustration had built to a boil, aggravated by two failed turnaround efforts at the beginning of the Kasim Reed administration. By 2015 Mayor Reed was impatient for real change. He brought in Tim Keane, the renowned former director of planning from Charleston, South Carolina, to lead a reform effort and used a grant from the local business group, the Atlanta Committee for Progress, to bring in an outside consulting expert, Mike Brink, to provide a plan.

Rather than a drawn-out process, Keane called for a full set of action items within six months. The starting point for Brink was the customers. There was a keen awareness that if the system were to change it had to be clearly and directly informed by the employers and home-owners who were most frustrated with standard operating procedures. As the outside advisers diligently interviewed a wide swath of customers and heard essentially the same tales of unending processes and poor service, they realized that no matter who was engaging with the system, there was the same reported bad experience.

Next was a careful breakdown of all work processes to identify the bottlenecks. Finally, a private company, SAFEBuilt, was brought in to develop highly detailed workflows and individualized permit plans that revolutionized the agency almost overnight.

The key insight was that Atlanta's building department needed to move away from its approach to permitting, which put every applicant into the same line without distinguishing between specific issues or different types of situations. In the old system, a staff person could conceivably start her morning with a request to repaint a house in a historic district, get the paperwork to build a forty-story office tower on Peachtree Street at noon, and finish the day with a request from a plumber to change a sewer line. Within months, city staff were shifted from being generalists to being assigned specific permit types. That's made a big difference; the details and technical specifications of a house-painting request are quite different than a permit to build an office tower. Now administrators can build up expertise, which makes everything work quicker.

Inspectors also know now that they have just one opportunity to make comments on a permit request and should aim to make the second review the last one. To ensure that happens, the city closely tracks the percentage of permits that are addressed in two looks. "The change to the two-look process made all the difference. It completely changed the incentive structure, and now everyone was focused on getting to 'yes' no matter how complicated the request was," says the outside expert Mike Brink.

The system includes at least a dozen other changes that all revolve around the user experience. A concierge service, for example, modeled on the Apple Store experience, includes a greeter to meet applicants as they walk into the Office of Buildings and personally usher them to the right people, with a goal (increasingly met) of having a customer out of the office within thirty minutes. There is also a newly hired customer advocate committed to continuing the process of translating customer feedback into operational change.

The results have been striking. From 2015 to 2016, the rating of customer satisfaction jumped 50 percent. A lot of this comes down to core process improvements. The workstream system the city has put in place reduced handoffs significantly. The express work stream (for simple permit requests) now handles 40 percent of the permit volume with an average processing time of thirty minutes. So instead of routing fairly straightforward permits past multiple individuals, they are handled in a single visit by a single person using the city's Accela cloud-based technology system. "It really just came down to thinking about the customer's interest every time we came together to discuss the process. It's so easy in government to forget the perspective of those outside the system and to accept as 'givens' pieces of the process that really don't make sense or add value," Keane says.

Atlanta's commitment to reform based on the needs of the customer and the importance of time and data can go even further. Future actions could include using mobile devices to provide better information to field inspectors and using analytics to better evaluate the risk of a certain set of plans, at a site, or from doing business with a certain developer.

Recognizing and Regulating Risk

The central concept that motivates regulation is assessing risk. The work of a vigilant building department is aimed at avoiding injuries by addressing the risk of unsafe structures or dangerous activities. In the abstract, the most certain way to prevent these risks is to issue no building permits at all. After all, no job sites means no construction workers to be injured. Yet clearly that is absurd. So the questions become: What level of risk do we find acceptable? And how do we effectively and efficiently regulate the mix of risk (injury) and reward (new buildings)?

When cities and states wrote most of their administrative procedures, someone who got sick from a restaurant could not Yelp about the experience. The city official processing a building permit could not instantly access information about previous projects of the company or its officers. A homeowner wishing to complain about shoddy electrical work by a contractor couldn't tweet a picture of the work to the city and neighbors.

Lacking the tools to have a detailed understanding of specific risks for specific situations, cities and states depended on broad, credential-based approaches—take a test, wait, get a license, go to work. Apply for a permit to open a business, visit a dozen city agencies, file the plans, wait, get an occupancy permit. Inspectors received assignments based on a list from every applicable project or business, not the most dangerous.

Today everything about how we can develop knowledge has changed, but little about how we regulate has. To reassess how cities should approach regulation, first they need to reassess risk. The federal government has a special White House office assigned to examine the benefits and costs of new regulations, the Office of Information and Regulatory Affairs. Few local and state offices have the capacity to undertake the complex economic studies commissioned by that office, but distributed, open governance can provide many of the answers.

No amount of traditional regulatory scrutiny, no matter how long it takes, will produce a system devoid of accidents. Some taxi driver will run into a pedestrian; some beautician will use the wrong hair dye; some restaurant will mislabel its fish. Risk underwriting depends on many varied factors, including frequency and severity of the potential harm. If the damage to a customer is low, the city may decide not to regulate, especially if the enforcement cost is high. There are certain situations where local and state government plays no role because the commercial activity is viewed as a minimal risk with relatively little potential damage. For example, one might need an occupancy license to open a bike store, but the city doesn't require a special license to sell bicycles. Federal laws protect consumers by mandating minimum safety requirements for the products, and competition in the marketplace ensures that overcharging or poor service is punished with fewer customers, less profit, and, if continued, a closed store.

Conversely, as referenced by Bryant Cannon and Hanna Chung at the California Department of Justice, "Government should take a more significant role in regulating activities where a failed transaction implies irreversible high-risk consequences."[9] For example it's important to require and inspect emergency door exits at theaters because if an audience can't easily get out in case of a fire many lives can be lost. Although a theater fire might be a rare event, the damage is too horrific to leave open even a small opportunity.

More data and better analytics allow cities to understand risk better, in more granular detail and much more deeply, about any specific entity or action. With more precise targeting of risk and the cost of regulation, cities can be more confident in moving away from the one-size-fits-all rules that throw up hurdles a potential operator must clear to go into a business or renovate a building or start a professional career.

The new regulators can use data secured from distributed sources to monitor risks, identifying, for example, the types of equipment or vehicles most likely to cause accidents.[10] Mobile tools could then provide suggestions based on this analysis to inspectors who will receive and transmit information about these issues in real time. City IoT sensors that report noise and air violations in the vicinity of an establishment can be integrated into a data-smart regulatory regime. If a nightclub is blaring music at four a.m. sensors can alert authorities in real time and document the problem for possible subsequent sanctions.

A version of what sensors can provide is happening in New York City, which has regulations that require landlords to meet minimum temperature standards for their tenants in the winter. HeatSeek, a project from the New York City BigApps contests, works with public interest attorneys, community-based organizations, and the NYC Department of Housing Preservation and Development (HPD) to install web-connected temperature sensors in apartments of tenants who want to document how low the temperature in their unit dips. Heat Seek web applications analyze the data and display it on an hourly graph and a heat log, giving tenants proof of problems when in negotiations with the landlord and, if it comes to it, in housing court.[11]

The process of connecting past history to new permit issuance can be complicated, however. Several years ago, New York City sought to stop issuing building permits to developers that owed money to the city. The effort failed because the two departments, Buildings and Finance, could not find a way to identify whether the person with an outstanding obligation was the same person requesting a new permit. The differences in the data, along with missing links to metadata such as the relationships among shell companies, made a solution expensive and complex. While more sophisticated analytics may today be required to identify scofflaw problems, a focus on how city officials collect data will, over time, produce cleaner information and reduce the need for much of the auxiliary analytics work and expense now required for the CRM to drive deep change in organizational behaviors.

Better, Faster, Safer

The most important permit reform the New York City building department implemented was shockingly simple—a scanner placed on the counter for public use, along with an instruction that paper is no longer welcome here. Acting in time and paper just do not mix. Paper equals handoffs, which equals sequential processing, which equals wasted time. In a digital world, only a government uninterested in its residents forces them to find out which forms apply to their circumstances, to look up the information, and fill out the forms. The new O/S, always focused on UX and acting in time, asks a straightforward question—do you want a restaurant permit? If the answer is yes, then the city works behind the scenes to do the search of addresses, zoning, sewer permit, fire restrictions, and the lot, filling in forms automatically and catching issues along the way, to assist the consumer and regulator alike.

Reforms to regulation, when coupled with those that create a more data-driven workforce, produce other advantages. For example, many cities struggle with scheduling building inspectors—first the electrical, then the plumbing, then the fire, all of which add time and expense to the construction. With new data-driven support and virtual reality tools more inspectors can be generalists, speeding the process considerably.

"Reg✓"

One day in New York City Hall when he was deputy mayor, Goldsmith, frustrated with the steady barrage of complaints from contractors waiting for permits, requested representatives from each of the relevant agencies to work together four nights a week, each night in a different borough, until the waiting list of work was addressed. In his visits to those special evening sessions, he watched and talked to the city workers and the architects, builders, planners, and developers who filled the room. Everyone seemed to know the "good guys"—those whose plans and work always met standards—and for the most part they had a good idea of those who didn't. Plans came with architectural and engineering certifications, and the city officials knew on which of those certifications they could most routinely rely.

Regulators can neither gather nor depend on that kind of insider industry knowledge to change their approach. But with smart analytics to delve into the highly fragmented but valuable information available in a distributed system, regulators can perform what might be dubbed Reg✓, similar in concept to the TSA PreCheck. Before they arrive at the airport PreCheck customers have been vetted with a thorough examination of their past, which fits them into the low-risk category. For Reg✓ the integrated systems would check the applicant's history for violations, workplace injuries, consumer complaints, tax payment compliance, OSHA inspection, and other records that appear applicable to the case. Whether it's a permit to be issued or an inspection of a site the new O/S possesses the ability to detect anomalies and patterns.

Those who earn a Reg✓ pass would at least not have to figuratively take off their shoes; their plans would quickly go through the review equivalent of the x-ray process. In this regard, the regulating process incorporates the operating acting-in-time principles, where more of the routine work is off-loaded, allowing time-pressured employees to redirect their time to complex cases, whether complexity is defined by the scope of the project or the official record background of the applicant and any related companies. If done correctly, the underlying concept is sound: use information to allow public service workers to concentrate on review of the complex cases for permits and on those actors without good records.

Using data to reallocate work can also produce efficiencies in the inspection process. In this instance, grading with analytics can create not a faster lane but one with much more scrutiny. Chicago did just that with an analytics-driven plan to prevent foodborne illness.[12] As in almost every city, inspectors stretch to get to all the places that need review. In Chicago thirty-five or so inspectors annually check 15,000 restaurants and other food retailers, and had averaged a violation rate of about 15 percent for critical items that affect the likelihood of foodborne illness. Chicago needed a faster way to protect the public by minimizing the health risks from potentially inspection-violating establishments.

The answer came from the city's talented data analytics team, operating under the direction of its chief data officer Tom Schenk, which took on the task of identifying the places that posed the highest likelihood of health risks. Schenk recruited additional talent, reaching out to Civic Consulting Alliance, an organization that pairs corporations with Chicago city departments on meaningful pro bono projects; that partnership brought in Allstate's data science team, as well.

Schenk began by interviewing the public health inspectors about how they did their work. They then reviewed their inspection reports, as well as data such as 311 call center information, weather, and other information readily available from the city's open data portal. They found that a particular set of variables could serve as leading indicators to predict problems. These leading indicators, which included an establishment's prior violations, location of the establishments, nearby sanitation and garbage complaints, time since the last inspection, nearby burglaries, and temperature readings inside or out, led to an increased likelihood of a given establishment earning a critical violation.

Based on this information, the department created a system where inspectors prioritized the places the analytics team predicted as likely to earn a critical violation, a metric based on how many variables each establishment met. Using the forecast list instead of the more routine assignment process, inspectors were able to, on average, detect critical violations seven days earlier than they otherwise would have. These approaches, which combine information from distributed sources with sophisticated analysis, will dramatically change the very concept of regulation.

Even when problems are found, the city might determine the best choice is a positive intervention that assists them in mitigating the actions that cause the risk. For example Los Angeles recognized in its Systematic Code Enforcement Program, which won a 2005 Harvard Innovations in American Government Award, that many of the individuals receiving citations for housing code violations lacked the resources to fix up their homes—not all the violators were slumlords. That allowed the officials to establish assistance programs that proved more effective than citations.

In some systems the work of gathering data and making predictions involves the industry in a collaborative fashion. For example, every day the Federal Aviation Administration (FAA) attempts to eliminate risks that would endanger the public. "Our risk-based decision making initiative is all about how to use data to identify risks in [the] aviation system and to mitigate them. We do this in collaboration with industry—they share data with us and with their competitors," says FAA Administrator Michael Huerta. Moving information to the FAA inspectors in the field needs to be accompanied by careful training so that they feel comfortable looking for the safety exceptions, rather than following the routines. "It is also a big cultural change, and we are in the midst of building new organizational structures and compliance frameworks," he says.

Concurrent Permit Processing

Imagine there is a café owner in the Bronx who wants to open a spot for diners to eat on the sidewalk outside her small storefront. She's excited; it will allow her to seat another dozen paying customers, and she likes how it will add a bit of liveliness and charm to her block, as well. She doesn't know what she's in for. Depending on her plans, she needs to get through the state Liquor Authority and the corporate filing department of the state and the city departments of planning, finance, buildings, health and transportation, as well as the fire department. There is a sequence to many of these steps, further slowing her efforts.

In New York City more than a dozen agencies can easily be involved in granting permission, a paper-based system that requires time-consuming handoffs, as the permit seeker is responsible for going from office to office—except those with the resources to hire someone to take up that responsibility. Worse, the agencies' decisions often require circular stops. Our favorite story is the homeowner who wanted a curb cut for a garage. The Department of Transportation approved, but only for one very specific location—which happened to be a spot occupied by a tree that the Parks Department refused to allow to be cut down. Evidently the homeowner negotiated until the departments agreed to move the driveway entrance slightly if he also planted a replacement tree.

In the distributed, digital O/S, however, cities can launch concurrent processing. With readily available workflow automation and electronic document management systems, multiple agencies could work on the same permit at the same time while still respecting where each is in terms of critical decisions. A distributed system produces better results more quickly when it comes equipped with a backbone that eliminates the handoff delays associated with paper documents and separate offices.

The goal of these digital processes, however, should not be to automate unnecessary or obsolete rules and requirements. Cities should also organize a regulatory look back to consolidate and eliminate permits and needless rules that accrete over time.[13] The conversion to a new O/S represents an opportune time for rethinking obsolete or unnecessary approaches.

REGULATION IN A DISTRIBUTED WORLD

The shared economy is making cities rethink regulation. The thicket of municipal laws for operating a hotel clearly are not all applicable to a homeowner renting a floor of a two-story apartment a few nights a week— but does the city have no responsibility for health and safety of the guests or zoning concerns in this situation? The same goes for transportation network companies (TNCs) such as Uber and Lyft, which do not neatly fit under the onerous rules for taxi medallions but still must be responsible for the safety of thousands of passengers in a city each day.

In Chicago the city made the decision early to create TNC regulation that keeps the burden of barriers to entry for TNCs as low as possible. To ensure baseline safety standards for vehicles and drivers, regulators implemented a licensing process in late 2014. The traditional taxi exam at the time required workers to commute to a community college for six days and learn things like how to read a paper map. TNC training can be done on the phone at the driver's leisure; topics include specific ride-sharing rules, how to transport passengers safely, and access issues for people with disabilities. The city requires the exam but the TNC administers it, which works for both parties. Uber is also interested in incorporating training into the driver experience. Since all cars are GPS located, the company could potentially provide information to drivers as they encounter situations, which may be better for retention than traditional testing.

Chicago also requires TNC partners to run driver background checks and regularly inspect vehicles. Whereas city inspections are costly and wait times build up quickly, Uber has set up a number of Greenlight Hubs for vehicle inspections, where a driver can have his or her car approved cheaply and quickly. The city has licensed a number of other repair shops to perform these inspections, as well.

To minimize the risk of fraud, the city maintains wide discretion to review documentation, request data, and impose repercussions on rule breakers. Any person who provides false documentation is denied licensing and required to reimburse the city for any revenue generated under false licensing. The city also requires all drivers to post a 311 sticker on each vehicle so customers are aware they may contact the city directly with any complaints.

Not every state and city regulatory system for shared economy companies like Uber and Airbnb goes as smoothly as Chicago's rules for TNCs. In fact, homeowners and the home sharing platform HomeAway.com have brought a lawsuit against the city of Chicago for its regulatory approach to their industry, and litigation over the issue has been filed in San Francisco and Nashville, as well.[14]

Certainly, how and whether to regulate these shared economy providers is a genuine issue deserving thoughtful approaches. Perhaps hidden by the challenges of these new situations, however, are the opportunities they present, particularly around which regulatory principles government could apply in managing risk where broadly available consumer information exists.

Yelp and Angie's List collect users' ratings of a service and then visualize that data to inform the decisions of future consumers. Uber and Lyft ask their fares to rate the experience, then reflect the average previous experience of a driver to a would-be customer to make him or her more willing (or not) to accept that ride. Where the application in a market has sufficient use, its socializing of previous experiences in an open network provides vastly more information about a specific operator than ever before available. With that information directly in the hands of citizens they have a previously unavailable set of information to add to their knowledge of a situation to make decisions about their own health and safety. In these instances and many more the new regulator needs to consider how these powerful platforms augment or replace standard regulation. In other words a plumber may incur a small penalty from the city for failing to follow code in a home installation and/or he may suffer a large reputation penalty when the homeowner posts his concerns on Angie's List.

Many factors affect the risk calculations of municipal regulators as they consider potential harm, ease of access to the information by prospective consumers, and scale and accuracy of the reported information. In situations where such a social platform does not exist, the city could incorporate another layer of information from the open data available from engaged customers, who, essentially, can act as informal inspectors when they take pictures and report problems and infractions via social media and sites such as Yelp.

The distributed system allows government to blend regulatory approaches from the traditional to co-regulated service. On one end of the continuum advocates defend the status quo with its regulations that use permission-based, lengthy screenings of proposed service providers as the only path to reducing bad actions. Other advocates propose easy entry that comes with wide reporting and, sometimes, with punishments for certain types of subsequent violations.

Florian Saurwein, senior scientist at the Institute for Comparative Media and Communication Studies, explores what he calls co-regulation and self-regulation to address these issues, advocating for new modes of governance that do not rely on command-and-control legal sanctions. "At the implementation stage [this open method uses] nonhierarchical and less formal modes of steering based on the creation of incentive structures, mutual learning, arguing and persuasion, and non-legal sanc-

TABLE 4-2 *Characteristics of a New Regulatory Model*

TRADITIONAL MODEL	OPEN METHOD
Restricts access to achieve policy goals (public safety, etc.)	Relaxes market access and then uses real-time data to hold actors accountable
Closed system	Open networks
Point to point: a complaint registered by a consumer to the city	Broadcast: good or bad experience with a service sent to many
Professional: depends on highly trained city inspectors	Casual: includes consumers, in part or exclusively
Avoids all risk: attempts through careful credentialing to eliminate risk	Learns from mistakes: in situations where the event would not be serious, reduces front-end screening
Compliance depends on inspection	Compliance depends at least in part on certification and disclosure

tioning methods such as naming and shaming."[15] In a paper written for the Smith-Richardson Regulatory Reform project at Harvard, Nick Grossman, now a senior adviser to a fund specializing in platform investments, sets out the distinction between the two approaches, which we modify and summarize in table 4-2.

Yet the choices presented by Grossman and Saurwein do not have to be binary. Cities with the new O/S can secure the best of each model, with a blend that depends on the industry to be regulated. No single answer will apply to all types of businesses or consumer interactions. All regulated commercial activities involve some "co-regulation," in the sense that businesses value their reputations as well as the costs associated with bad or harmful services or products. Therefore, the emerging regulatory questions revolve around that balance.

To determine how to strike the balance municipalities can use a distributed system that incorporates data analytics and social media from licensed providers of services. In considering how to determine the right regulatory balance between traditional and open for an industry or activity, cities could apply the following criteria:

1. Evaluate the type of information recorded by third-party providers and how broadly available it is to consumers.

2. Obtain assurance that the third party has committed to broadly acquiring and verifying the accuracy of the relevant data that will be supplied to consumers.

3. Establish that the system can collect a sufficient number of ratings of high enough quality that providers or competitors would not be able to game the results.

4. Determine minimum standards of conduct that set the foundation, after which the reputational ratings would encourage performance exceeding mere compliance.

These criteria highlight an additional important point: in many cases permitting is a design relic of an outdated credentialing system. Permits represent one way to control behaviors. Yet design thinking combined with data mining allows officials to set standards of conduct— codes—and identify attributes of the citizen/business that determine its likelihood to comply. Forcing the business to apply for a permit or license is more than just slow and expensive; it will increasingly become unnecessary and an inferior way to guarantee safety.

Reputational Ratings: Distributed Enforcement

Newer approaches to protecting health and safety do not rely so much on traditional credentialing but, instead, add or substitute reputational ratings. These approaches augment traditional city approaches or even replace them. In any of these scenarios, the distributed system heavily involves the role of consumers. We look at these options not so much in terms of whether government should legislate or whether plumbers should self-regulate but more as a blend that can be varied, determined by risk.

Because these new modes of regulation involve more social action and less hierarchical command-and-control action they allow a business to enter the market more quickly. This distributed system facilitates more variety in the regulatory programs and reduces the barriers to entry for small businesses and new businesses with innovative products.

One reason these tools work in certain shared economy situations such as with Uber, Lyft, and Airbnb is because the consequences of the risks are low and the amount of socially available information is great. In these situations, government should still propose standards, but ease the barriers to entry and speed the results with lighter touches. Officials can use these new tools to produce sufficient safety in a distributed system, reducing costs of doing business in a city while concurrently gathering more information that will make the marketplace safer and more efficient.

Distributed "Inspecting"

In 2013 the City of San Francisco tried something new; it worked with Yelp to display health inspector ratings on restaurant pages alongside visitor ratings and comments. For years, professional public health departments resisted this integration, fearing that the judgment of their inspectors would lose value if presented alongside less formal responses from diners. Unlike an inspector's professional search for material infractions, foodborne illness may or may not be directly subject to a diner's observation. But there are thousands more diners than inspectors, and the warning signs to future customers from these customers might, indeed, be helpful.

Harvard Business School professor Michael Luca has researched Yelp restaurant comments and San Francisco health department ratings.[16] He found that customers make, if not good inspectors, at least good predictors of future events. With coauthor Yejin Choi, Luca used Yelp text and ratings and found that the Yelp reviews correctly classified more than 80 percent of restaurants; that is, the Yelp data identified the same bad actors as the inspectors who observe that their inspections are qualitatively different than those of a diner.

The Luca results demonstrate that the social information provides an invaluable additional source of information. Incorporating that "amateur" report does present challenges in terms of what should be reported and in what manner. Yet, as Luca notes, "restaurants whose low hygiene ratings are posted on Yelp tend to respond by cleaning up and performing better on their next inspections."[17] Luca's work underscores the critical point that transparently available information drives conduct. Most owners respond positively to restaurant grades; for example, cleaning up the shop to achieve a higher rating. This model could be used across all interventions. It would also alleviate some of the privacy, trust, and due process concerns, as the data would not be used for punitive measures but additive assistance.

Distributed Reporting

In another hybrid model the new O/S regulations can mitigate risk with wider distribution of information about company performance via social media and requirements that a company disclose certain events, with both placed on top of a regulatory floor that insures health and safety will be protected. In these instances city and state officials need to consider if and how this distributed reporting model adequately addresses a situation's specific risks to the public, as well as how much reputational ratings adequately influence marketplace transactions.

In "Outcome-Based Regulatory Strategies for Promoting Greater Patient Safety" Stephen Sugarman illustrates this blend of setting standards and requiring mandatory disclosure in his study of patient safety outcomes. He highlights the combination of what he calls two regulatory strategies, "disclosure" and "performance-based regulation," where the government holds regulated parties responsible for achieving targets measured in terms of safer outcomes.

The view that required disclosure alone could stimulate stronger market pressures toward greater patient safety rests on twin beliefs: first, with better information about results inserted into the marketplace, safer providers will gain a larger share of the healthcare business, thereby subjecting patients to a lower risk of avoidable adverse events; and second, out of fear of losing patients to those safer providers, the currently less-safe providers will improve their performance, which will also benefit patients. Performance-based regulation assumes that competition for business will itself not suffice to bring about the optimal level of patient safety and that healthcare providers must be directly prodded by government with penalties and/or rewards to achieve safer outcomes.[18]

These approaches enhance the likelihood that valuable information will arrive in time to a potential customer or give an official time to act when a problem occurs. Well-organized information collected continuously from distributed sources—in this case both from customers and the business itself—will replace inspection that relies on a limited number of inspectors who disrupt the business of honest merchants in a needle-in-a-haystack quest to find material violations. The penalties and rewards that Sugarman suggests can vary by industry and the specifics of circumstances.

A version of this model is incorporated into how Chicago is regulating TNCs, alongside its other requirements. Once the city has ensured baseline safety standards for a driver, it then utilizes the internal customer feedback systems of the TNC to identify unsafe drivers and driving practices. Each TNC must have in place a process to notify the city or trigger an inspection when any driver receives complaints that give rise to public safety concerns or if their app rating falls below a certain threshold. If a customer complaint leads to the firing of a driver for an illegal activity, the TNC is required to make the driver's information known to the city within forty-eight hours. The city may then request drug testing and physical examination of the driver in question.

Chicago's hybrid system has ensured customer safety but kept obstacles for becoming a driver to a minimum, in part by speeding the process by getting out of the way. Private companies, which have strong motivation to have drivers on the road and working as quickly as they can, are the responsible party for monitoring the safety of their affiliated drivers and vehicles, and government maintains its responsibility for health and safety through the burden of disclosure.

For this type of program to work well it also requires a distributed operating system that enables the city to gather information from multiple sources and organize it in a way that can create reputational pressure. A marketplace only functions well when information is accessible and reliable. Some actors will over-perform because it's in their culture and because it produces new business, while others may have failures, some of which affect health and safety and result in fines.

CITY AS REFEREE IN THE INFORMATION GAME

This chapter presents two principles concerning regulation. First, there is a continuum of regulatory options, from no involvement to heavy permission-based involvement. Second, a distributed approach that broadly facilitates the exchange of data will be of benefit to government and consumers alike, help identify risk much more quickly, and speed all the formal related actions.

In this continuum there will be situations where the time and trouble and benefit of inspecting creates more cost to the city and the consumer than the effort warrants. For example, authors Bryant Cannon and Hanna Chung write, "The purse-sharing economy of Bag Borrow or Steal involves the sharing of a relatively low-risk commodity—luxury purses that cost around a few hundred to rent by the month. If a consumer damages the purse, the insurance policy anticipates the risk."[19] The need for city inspectors and regulations would not be worth the cost of the effort in this kind of instance.

At the same time, when considering opportunities for third-party certification models, cities must understand that reputation systems face the limitations referenced previously, including the issue of confidence that there are a sufficient number of reports of high enough quality to assist the consumer. A prospective consumer considers various factors when choosing a store or product, including the number. These observations can help government collect, organize, and distribute information that informs customers and, in turn, enhances fairness and safety, irrespective of the enforcement regime itself.

The role of government in vouching for information has long been important. Government makes sure the rules create a fair playing field so that a consumer can rely on pricing information. City Hall weights and measures offices undertook this responsibility a century ago, making sure the butcher's scale adequately read a pound of meat and, later, that the gas station pump really dispensed a gallon, as it claimed. Even here there are questions of how to best fulfill this duty. How often does the city need to send Joe from Weights and Measures to the gas station to inspect their equipment? When does a social platform with thousands of comments suffice as information that can be shared, and under what set of rules?

A city can also provide an invaluable service to its citizens by making it easy to access and understand the information it possesses. For example, by adding its data to other information from multiple sources, a city site could assist a family with a complex decision, such as choosing a Pre-K provider. Today, to consider many factors, the family might need to find health and safety information on the city's website, data on quality from state childcare ratings, and parental comments from various social media sources. When all that information (and more) is easier to access, simpler to understand, and from a trusted site, the consumer is better off—and the noncompliant schools have more pressure to improve.

Of course a system that relies on reputation and trust will still need to impose penalties for infractions that escalate, depending on the seriousness of the infraction or the extent to which the violation undermines the integrity of the system. For example, a false reporting or certification undermines the underlying principles of trust in the ratings that assist the consumer and would deserve serious consequences.

As cities consider changing regulations in any of these ways, they can and should use the new open government framework and systems to include citizen input. Governments regularly post proposed regulations in a digital format for comment, but it is much less frequent that they explain the issue in a way that informs the public of the options and solicits stakeholder feedback before the rule is even suggested. A comprehensive outreach strategy will produce suggestions about solutions as well as inform the city of unintended consequences. Because the system is open and distributed those who comment will also respond to each other's posts, and the city can iterate the discussion by adding questions until it gets enough information to propose a rule or ordinance, which will then go through the same process.

The sea change in resources available to regulators in a new O/S shows the opportunities and challenges. The issue is not a simple binary one, such as does a city regulate a shared economy provider like Airbnb or Uber or not. Rather the true opportunity involves how government incorporates the best of a reputation-based system with or instead of older forms of more detailed and cumbersome regulation. The new O/S, however, provides an opportunity and framework that presents the distributed regulatory framework as relevant, regardless of the nature of the service.

A distributed operating system will enhance timely regulatory responses, weaving together a much broader array of information to identify safety and consumer fraud issues sooner, to preempt harm, and to operate quicker with confidence on behalf of reputable businesses. More distributed sources of information, identified and organized quickly with machine learning and analytics, can both speed the opening of a business and speed awareness of a problem somewhere else.

Chapter 4   THE BOTTOM LINE

Key Points

- Government has long been constructed as a highly routinized organization, slow to change with shifting conditions and circumstances. A new digital O/S is agile and responds in time with rapid-cycle processes that produce dramatic benefits.

- Few areas demonstrate the need to act in time as much as regulation. Whether obtaining a permit or license or passing an inspection, local government continues to use check-the-box protocols and systems that cost citizens money and time.

- Regulation is essentially about assessing risk, but the old systems lack the precise tools to discern the different risks in each circumstance.

- Using new technology and a distributed approach local government can identify risk more accurately and sooner, dramatically saving time and improving health outcomes for citizens.

- The new O/S calls for a pivot from uniform approaches to a quicker system based on new data analytic tools that can identify where to look for problems, new automating data sources, new ways to concurrently work on requests across agencies, and new ways to support frontline workers making decisions without slow approval processes.

Pitfalls

- Regulatory processes must periodically be reviewed, as some are captive to strong interest groups that create barriers to entry.

- Regulations set too high and too onerous will foster noncompliance.

Recommendations

- Cities should apply a metric of elapsed time spent.

- Institute a new system called Reg✓, based on TSA PreCheck, that evaluates those seeking permits so official reviewers can fast track those with good histories and less complex requests.

- Consider various opportunities to blend a hybrid of existing regulations with reputation-based sharing economy information sources.

Examples

- In just one year Atlanta shrunk wait times and doubled customer satisfaction of its building permitting process by analyzing workflows and holding government staff accountable to strict outcome measures such as limiting permit requests to a two-step approval process.

- Chicago used data analytics to accurately predict potential sites of foodborne illness. This allowed the city's small team of restaurant inspectors to prioritize establishments most likely to receive a violation rather than the typical routine assignment process that yielded far fewer infractions.

NOTES

1. Benjamin Franklin, "Poor Richard Improved, 1748," *National Archives: Founders Online* (https://founders.archives.gov/documents/Franklin/01-03-02 -0103).

2. Shanker Ramamurthy, "Speed to Insight: Key to Big Data Success," *Information Week*, January 2015 (www.informationweek.com/big-data/big-data -analytics/speed-to-insight-key-to-big-data-success/a/d-id/1318449).

3. James Hodson, "How to Make Your Company Machine Learning Ready," *Harvard Business Review*, November 2016 (https://hbr.org/2016/11 /how-to-make-your-company-machine-learning-ready).

4. Katherine Hillenbrand, "New Orleans Brings Data-Driven Tools to Blight Remediation," *Data-Smart City Solutions*, October 12, 2016 (http://datasmart .ash.harvard.edu/news/article/new-orleans-brings-data-driven-tools-to-blight -remediation-915).

5. Tibi Puiu, "Your Smartphone Is Millions of Times More Powerful Than All of NASA's Combined Computing in 1969," *ZME Science*, May 17, 2017 (www.zmescience.com/research/technology/smartphone-power-compared-to -apollo-432).

6. Drake Baer, "How Airbnb Solved the Mystery of Predictive Pricing," *Fast Company*, February 2014 (www.fastcompany.com/3026550/how-airbnb -solved-the-mystery-of-predictive-pricing).

7. Andrew Maier, "Paper, Cut: The Bleeding Edge Of Government Forms," *1 Civic Quarterly*, Fall 2014.

8. "The Regulatory Reform for the 21st Century City Project," *Data-Smart City Solutions*, 2014 (http://datasmart.ash.harvard.edu/regulation).

9. Bryant Cannon and Hanna Chung, "A Framework for Designing Co-Regulation Models Well-Adapted to Technology-Facilitated Sharing Economies," *Santa Clara High Tech Law Journal* 31 (January 2014), p. 73.

10. See GeoHub (http://geohub.lacity.org).

11. See Heat Seek (http://heatseek.org/how-it-works-2).

12. Sean Thornton, "Delivering Faster Results with Food Inspection Forecasting: Chicago's Analytics-Driven Plan to Prevent Foodborne Illness," *Data-Smart City Solutions*, May 19, 2015 (http://datasmart.ash.harvard.edu/news /article/delivering-faster-results-with-food-inspection-forecasting-631).

13. Jennifer Baxter, Lisa Robinson, and James Hammitt, "White Paper: A Retrospective Benefit-Cost Analysis," *Data-Smart City Solutions*, April 20, 2015 (http://datasmart.ash.harvard.edu/news/article/white-paper-retrospective -benefit-cost-analysis-665).

14. Ally Marotti, "Homeaway Lawsuit Alleges Chicago's 'Deeply Flawed' Home-Sharing Law is Unconstitutional," *Chicago Tribune*, May 23, 2017.

15. Florian Saurwein, "Regulatory Choice for Alternative Modes of Regulation: How Context Matters," *Law and Policy* 33 (July 2011), p. 36.

16. Michael Luca and others, "Where Not to Eat? Improving Public Policy by Predicting Hygiene Inspections Using Online Reviews," *EMNLP* (October 2013), pp. 1443–48.

17. Michael Luca and Luther Lowe, "City Governments Are Using Yelp to Tell You Where Not to Eat," *Harvard Business Review*, February 12, 2015 (https://hbr.org/2015/02/city-governments-are-using-yelp-to-tell-you-where-not-to-eat).

18. Stephen D. Sugarman, "Outcome-Based Regulatory Strategies for Promoting Greater Patient Safety," *Theoretical Inquiries in Law* 15 (July 2014), p. 580.

19. Cannon and Chung, "A Framework for Designing Co-Regulation Models," p. 64.

FIVE

The Problem-Solving Public Servant

Distributed governance transforms public employees from rule-bound workers to professionals who have the discretion, capacity, and authority to craft responses that better and more quickly solve problems in the city. Under the new O/S, the city tells street paving crews that their goal is no longer just to fill potholes; now they should be thinking about everything it takes to provide drivers with smooth streets. When crews have the discretion to make their own choices about how to expend effort—does this block need a few cracks filled or is it time to invest in preventive maintenance to prevent worse damage—they will accomplish more.

To give employees that power and expect them to be successful, cities and counties will have to use technologies now available, from novel data sources to dashboards, in a systematic, purposeful way. Yet the old operating systems of government—civil service, pay, procurement, budget priorities, and performance defined by compliance not outcomes—stand in the way. That means that technology is only one part of the picture. Cities also will have to change their thinking around credentials, procedures, reporting, and more. These changes will be met with resistance. As Donald Kettl, one of the leading academic experts on public management, notes about government:

> Much of the information collected simply goes to demonstrate compliance with rules rather than to improve the delivery of programs. A quick look at the information collected by government reveals that much of it supports box-checking compliance with government requirements. . . . For many players in government's world, that means information is often viewed as a gotcha game, to identify problems, or as defense against investigations, to minimize hassles. And that, in turn, makes it harder to convince all the players to use information to support positive steps like making programs work better, because many government insiders look on information with profound suspicion.[1]

With new technologies, however, come new ways to move beyond box-checking compliance yet still hold empowered employees accountable for results. Agency leaders have access to more real-time data, which allows them to keep track of how effective the paving crew is in meeting its broader new goals, to measure output in terms of smooth streets, and to monitor where they have been working over the course of the workday. Using data to manage accountability extends not just to outcomes but also to ensuring protection of democratic norms of integrity, fairness, and equity, which play a particularly important part in jobs such as social worker, police officer, and teacher. Here, too, the new O/S can use data and systems to judge whether discretion is being used wisely.

By moving to a system that provides public servants with the information and the autonomy to make decisions, have a voice in how their department approaches its goals, and work with other departments at City Hall and other institutions in the city, the new O/S is rewriting the job description of a municipal employee. In a virtuous circle, that increases the job satisfaction and effectiveness of these employees, making them better at their jobs and more trusted by the city's citizens.

ALLEGHENY COUNTY'S EMPOWERED CASEWORKERS

Marc Cherna has the mixture of optimism and frustration that comes from years of facing long odds and maneuvering around bureaucratic obstacles to win important battles for children. Cherna started as a youth worker forty years ago and now serves as the director of the Allegheny County Department of Human Services (DHS), responsible for publicly funded services in Pittsburgh and more than one hundred other contiguous municipalities. (In most of the United States, county governments provide social and health services, although in several places, like New York City and San Francisco, city and county governments are merged.) From his efforts Cherna has obtained a sort of public sector Holy Grail: a data warehouse that brings together information from twenty-nine different criminal justice, education, and human service sources. Only one other local government in the country has done something similar, and for not nearly as long as Allegheny County has had its system in place.

More than just an accomplishment for IT staff, integrated data—coupled with smart UX designed with the county's child welfare caseworkers in mind—is literally saving and improving lives. Now, thanks to cloud computing, data mining, and analytics, when a caseworker in Allegheny County enters a home in response to a call alleging abuse or neglect to meet with an often emotional, sometimes angry family, she is a skilled knowledge worker supported by the best practices and vast amounts of well-visualized data from predictive, community, and third-party sources. One resource, the system's Client View, provides data insights on DHS clients, such as history of involvement with the child welfare, mental health, jail, and public housing systems, and the caseworker knows which other government programs have been used by the family beyond this core information, as well.

Back at the office, caseworkers receive alerts about changes in the circumstances of families in their caseload; whether a child under supervision was suspended from school, for example, or when there is a birth into a home already involved with child welfare due to abuse. Client View in Allegheny County follows in the footsteps of Casebook, a program funded by the Annie E. Casey Foundation, an Internet-based application that gives caseworkers tools and cross-agency data in an easy-to-use dashboard.

Because life and technology move faster than government, Cherna could meet his goals of an effective, efficient, and data driven/informed system by mastering what other savvy public leaders have had to learn, the work around. He was helped by changes that occurred when he started working in Allegheny County. In 1997 the county government was completely reformed by referendum, collapsing the three-commissioner system to one with a single chief executive, and merging twenty-six different agencies into five. Cherna took over the newly created Department of Human Services, a sort of superagency that included formerly discrete social services functions.

Cherna reached out to the community and local foundations for assistance knowing that DHS could not create an integrated human services system alone and solely with government funding. Most of the major local philanthropies created an Integration Fund, managed by The Pittsburgh Foundation, which was dedicated to advancing innovation for human services, with support for research and development around new efforts for integrated data playing a pivotal role. This was an unusual stroke of luck and a clear demonstration of Cherna's ability to work collaboratively with community partners; philanthropies rarely work in concert around issues of data and government agency coordination. At the beginning, Deloitte was hired to build out the initial data warehouse framework and clarify how best to use advanced technology. Later funds supported analysis of work and time flows, which are critical to effectively integrating data and related services.

"This was all work for which we could never have received support from traditional government sources. They were funds that could be used to try out new, ambitious approaches. Some didn't work out, but if they did and we had the data to prove it, he [Cherna] would always find a way to permanently support the work with government dollars," says Erin Dalton, who leads the data team at DHS.

Cherna also understands that human services funding provides limited resources to hire individuals with the expertise to use such technology and analyze data optimally. As with most local government HR systems, there tends to be a long, confusing hiring period and then little flexibility in terms of pay scale and job description. To address these issues, DHS contracted with a nonprofit agency specializing in contracted personnel to locate the technical expertise needed. This agency makes the application process simple and, because it is the employer rather than DHS, it can set wages, job descriptions, and promotion standards that match industry standards for data analytics.

Fortunately Pittsburgh is home to Carnegie Mellon University and the University of Pittsburgh, two of the best data analytics training grounds in the country. Both provide excellent pools of analytics candidates. DHS representatives make a point of reaching out to these and other local university students and exposing them to county government long before they graduate, offering them internships and other opportunities to demonstrate their skills.

"Most [of our recruits] never thought of a government job before. Your average student, let alone one focused on analytics, would not have the patience required for applying for a government job, for taking a civil service exam and the general opaque process of government hiring," Dalton notes.

DHS is seeing concrete improvements because of its new data-driven/informed methods. For example, the Allegheny County child welfare and school systems now share data about school mobility for children who are in the child welfare system, and that measure shows that school switches have dropped 20 percent between 2005 and 2009. That's an important outcome for student education; it is well-known that a child's academic performance is adversely impacted when he or she changes school—even more so if it happens because of a home removal.[2]

A testament to the success of Cherna's technology-rooted approach is that other county departments have turned to him for help. Criminal justice agencies responsible for managing incarceration and probation data wanted to be able to access the DHS Data Warehouse, for instance, and Cherna was happy to oblige. Success begets success. As more agencies trust the data they add their information to the system, as well, providing even more information that can be integrated into the Data Warehouse and used to improve people's lives.

KEY COMPONENTS OF A DATA-INFUSED SYSTEM

The child welfare system connects with families, schools, healthcare workers, criminal justice officials, and a cast of private-sector neighbors and friends. It's far from unique, though. From providing health care to crime reduction, local government interacts with a wide network of individuals and organizations. According to University of Albany professor J. Ramon Gil-Garcia, "The next ten years could witness the emergence of a highly integrated virtual State in which all branches of government and multiple social actors seamlessly interact through the use of sophisticated technologies that integrate business processes, physical infrastructure, organizational resources, and new institutional arrangements."[3]

The new O/S requires authorities to mine information languishing in large legacy and affiliated third-party systems, sensor data generated by IoT networks, social media, smartphone photos submitted by engaged residents, and insights produced from machine-read documents. The constant flow of data from all these diverse sources will be a nearly useless cacophony of noise, however, without a new mechanism to integrate, analyze, and present the data to public servants who are trained to use it.

That mechanism is a socio-technical ecosystem comprised of 1) trusted social networks, 2) shared information, 3) integrated data, and 4) an interoperable technical infrastructure.[4] Together, these elements allow government to preemptively solve problems, re-imagine the roles and responsibilities of frontline workers and their managers and support, and successfully operate a distributed governance model. The innovative approach does not use IT systems for simple transaction processing. It unlocks the data hidden in those digital file cabinets, layers it with information derived from other sources, and applies algorithms to offer new answers and opportunities. This chapter discusses what it takes to create such a system and the internal opportunities it presents for public servants. Chapter 6 will explore how the same system can unlock the potential in distributed governance of external third parties involved in delivering public services.

Leadership to Create Collaboration

Ask almost anyone in the public sector the key change ingredient for nearly any issue and "leadership" will be the response. It may be a cliché, but to establish a socio-technical ecosystem the first answer of what it takes to be successful is leadership. A new O/S will drive an outcome-oriented strategy across agencies and down through the bureaucracy, and that requires a leader who articulates a bold vision.

Because the new O/S is a significant break with the past, the responsibility for championing the O/S lies with the top elected official and the designated persons to whom he or she delegates responsibility. In New York City current endeavors that would be a precursor to a new O/S are helmed by a deputy mayor and the director of operations with responsibility for cross-city data projects. In other locales, like Kansas City, it is the mayor and city manager. Leadership at the top is tasked with not only replacing old forms of practice but also, because the distributed system requires tight control of public priorities, establishing metrics to determine whether those priorities are being advanced, and determining the rules and regulations that insure fairness in the day-to-day work.

Senior executives—mayor, county executive, city manager, agency chief—produce results when their articulated vision is understood and realized by public employees and engaged communities. This requires attention to all three elements in figure 5-1: a vision (what are the key priorities), engagement (how are residents and relevant stakeholders involved in the process), and distributed operations (agencies, staff, and external partners that can produce the results). It could be argued that these elements can and should be essential elements to be considered for any large government project or program. Because action and discretion will no longer be isolated at the top rungs of government in distributed governance, however, leadership needs to clearly express itself in strategic choices and tangible action that guides the networked delivery system.

It is worth noting, in particular, the critical importance of government consciously establishing engagement opportunities within city

FIGURE 5-1   *Elements to Establish a New O/S*

government among frontline workers and externally with civic partners, including citizens. In the past, change powered almost exclusively by mayoral vision may have been sufficient. In the new O/S, city leadership must also articulate an engagement (UX) strategy and follow through with it. Even some of the country's best-known mayors, including Rahm Emanuel in Chicago and Bill de Blasio in New York, have occasionally found their vision stymied by residents who felt left out of the process. Outreach needs to include a broad and deep-seated commitment to involve residents and frontline workers throughout policymaking and implementation. This should not be akin to a corporation appointing a diversity officer or a police department adding one community policing officer and thinking it has checked off the community policing box. Cities need to craft new, broader approaches to engagement and cocreation that leverage social media and other communications tools to reach more individuals in more communities.

With the elements of vision, engagement, and operations in mind, leadership in the city will need specific programs and plans to institute the new O/S. The implementation guide appendix "Strategies to Address the Ten Most Important Challenges to a New O/S" provides a checklist of possible challenges to establishing distributed governance in a city, as well as core ideas that will allow local government to effectively address those issues.

Other resources exist that also can provide leaders with ideas and options for implementation. For instance Equipt to Innovate, launched by Living Cities in 2016, is a framework for cities to build toward what they call high-performance government. It offers a handful of specific outcomes for seven key elements of urban government—from forming broad partnerships to strategically deploying resources. The framework is especially useful as a resource during operationalizing a new O/S because several of its categories match the central ideas of this book, such as building employee engagement and considering the appropriate use of data, as well as an emphasis on integrating changes. "Within the overarching vision, all other city plans (comprehensive, transportation, sustainability, resiliency, etc.) [should be] well-sequenced and coordinated," Living Cities explains.[5]

These approaches by necessity require using digital tools in new ways. Technology does not solve all problems, but it is the key nutrient that will make the entire system work. Practically speaking this means that traditional IT shops must be transformed into running or supporting the city's knowledge management plan. These responsibilities can be found under relatively new job titles, like analytics officer, chief innovation officer, or chief data officer, or more established posts, such as chief information officer or chief of staff. Louisville, for example, began its reforms with extraordinarily qualified individuals in separate innovation and performance offices and eventually merged the offices.

Those carrying the banner for change face a difficult battle. The elected official can help those he designates to lead that effort by insuring that the other critical components of government get the message as well and become part of the solution. Scott Cordes in St. Paul, Minnesota, makes this clear:

I started out as the Mayor's budget guy. Then we wanted to engage in more data-driven innovation. Well, rather that have that take place in another office we realized they should be one and the same. I mean if our budget isn't innovative then what will be? I also realized that this can transform how all our workers approach their jobs. As a budget director, I don't hear about innovation until after it's too late and we must make cuts, but with the imperative to improve operations all the time, we are now asking our agencies and their staff to be innovative at the front end—in effect pushing innovation all the way down the system.

In Illinois, then incoming governor of Illinois Bruce Rauner pledged to apply his business experience to a state government badly in need of modernization, including setting up the Department of Innovation and Technology. He appointed Hardik Bhatt, who had a private-sector background in smart city technology as well as experience as Chicago's CIO and chief digital officer. When Bhatt started in 2015, Illinois had outdated hardware and software, few enterprise contracts, and no analytics group. Under Bhatt's leadership, and with the deputy governor as his partner, the state consolidated thirty-eight data silos, identifying key performance indicators and clustering IT work to bring agencies together around common problems.

Establishing a Socio-Technical Ecosystem

Despite the need for some central role office to drive change, the new O/S is not a centralized system. In fact, quite the opposite—the power of the O/S comes from creating an open system. We can see this vision emerging in Allegheny County, which recognizes that the information system needs to reflect the system in which an at-risk child lives. Various actors affect the child and produce data—from social workers who enter information in an IT system at her school to peers who might generate threatening, publicly-posted social media. With clear rules that govern the use of data around privacy, access, and technical protocols, this network of organizations can carefully turn the information into actionable knowledge for the responsible caseworker.

Many of the most difficult problems confronted by government could be represented by a diagram similar to figure 5-2—lots of actors employed or contracted by government touching the issue with little

FIGURE 5-2 *One Individual, Many Data Systems*

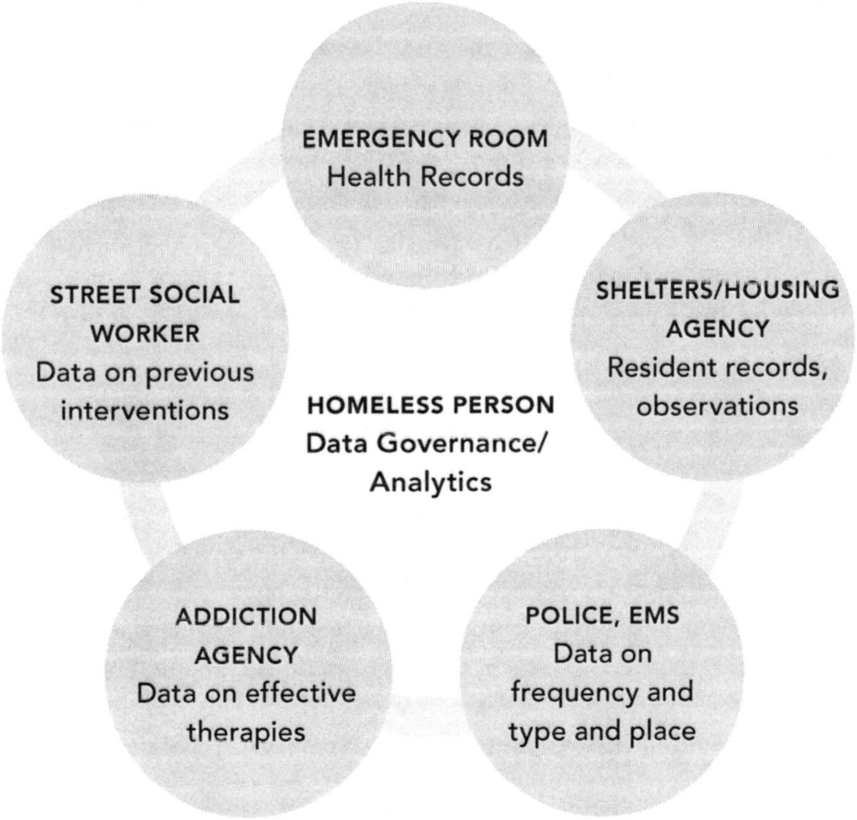

EMERGENCY ROOM
Health Records

STREET SOCIAL WORKER
Data on previous interventions

SHELTERS/HOUSING AGENCY
Resident records, observations

HOMELESS PERSON
Data Governance/ Analytics

ADDICTION AGENCY
Data on effective therapies

POLICE, EMS
Data on frequency and type and place

coordination. The issue of homelessness illustrates how critical data can be integrated as part of a treatment plan. In most current municipal models the information is fragmented, with one member of a completely unofficial network sharing data with one or more of the others only when a specific request is submitted. The goal of an O/S is to provide a governance and IT structure that allows integrated data across systems such as these. One can imagine each city agency creating a custom set of the information it needs, as well as producing real-time dashboards visualizing its performance, designed to highlight the most important metrics for its work. Further then, the data tools would allow officials to zoom in on those performance dashboards organized by district, supervisor, or whichever unit of analysis helps the most.

There must be an official and an office that owns the responsibility for supporting the data needs of city initiatives, whether that includes cross-agency work, performance (stat) units, or policy experts addressing systemic problems. In Illinois, the CIO and governor's office took an early and fundamental step when they established a data-sharing agreement that knocked down procedural and legal obstacles to cross-agency data sharing and collaboration. Bhatt summarized the scope of his office in pushing everything from analytics to human-centered design in various agencies:

> We also are driving data literacy in state government through our Analytics Center of Excellence. Representatives from various agencies meet every month to discuss best practices. And we also support innovation incubators for specific clusters, such as health and human services, public safety, business, and workforce. We literally have teams that are focusing on interoperability and data sharing, which started from the Health and Human Services transformation team. We basically are the service bureau, training center, and the center of excellence. We prioritize projects based on complexity, help the agencies understand complexity, and assist them with developing the business case and the tool set and infrastructure to build it.

In Los Angeles, Lilian Coral heads up a data team that has worked toward many of the same goals—with a twist. Since she is chief data officer for the city rather than a chief information officer, she doesn't have the authority or staff to require other departments to make changes, as Bhatt does. She spent months going from department to department creating enthusiasm and connections among the data and systems analysts in each agency.

"We realized we needed to create a community and tight relationships," Coral says. "I describe my team as a catalyst. The mayor is a great data champion and he sets the broad directive, but the goal is to have a decentralized approach to all our data work." The office supports regular citywide meetings of key personnel to share knowledge, identify citywide data needs and opportunities, and provide training and technical assistance. Coral's organizing work has been quite effective, as the relationships have stuck and led to significant culture change that has fostered more cross-departmental partnership.

The true pivot in Los Angeles toward an O/S took root when Coral's team established the GeoHub, the city's platform that allows anyone to explore, visualize, and download location-based open data, with the capacity to analyze and combine data using maps and to develop web and mobile applications. In addition to being open to the public, the Hub has capacities and connections designed specifically for city employees, accessed with a login. L.A. used a major licensing agreement with ESRI, the industry leader in digital mapping technology, to create the project, testament that there is no single blueprint for the sociotechnical ecosystem. The data office doesn't own the data in GeoHub, and it doesn't determine what any department submits. What it has done is set the rules of engagement so participation adds value, such as a uniform template that all incoming data must follow and rules for submitting data, including a requirement that departments must provide a contact for each dataset.

The hub model is one approach to sharing data across departments (and, as explored in greater depth in chapter 6, with external partners, as well). Another model can be for a Data Analytics Team like Coral's to set the rules of engagement—or protocols—for data sharing that L.A. has established for all participants, but not centralize where that data is available. In this model, if a manager at the Housing Department, for instance, would find it useful to add to her team's dashboard geocoded data from the Transportation Department about transit options and schedules, she would contact Transportation directly and have files that work flawlessly with her data the same afternoon. Data no longer needs to be isolated, but nor does it need to be centrally managed. It just needs to be able to cross departmental boundaries seamlessly.

As agencies drive performance through analysis—and as they add and train analysts—much of the intra-agency work and the tasks in table 5-1 will begin to be accomplished in the departments themselves, instead of the supporting Data Analytics Team. As data maturity grows,

TABLE 5-1 *Responsibilities of the Data Analytics Team*

TASK	ACTIVITIES OF THE ANALYTICS TEAM
Data Sharing Agreements	■ Establish executive order priorities and protocols for sharing data across departments.
Problem Identification	■ The performance culture should begin to understand the power of data and nominate problems for analysis and prioritization.
Business Process Analysis	■ Study the problem to be solved, identify the policy result to be achieved, and explain the challenge to the department responsible. ■ Clearly articulate the goals of the analytics project and how it will create benefit. ■ Interact with department end-users of analytics projects (many teams call this the "client-facing" role).
Data Analysis	■ Clean and normalize large datasets. ■ Perform analytics to identify trends and underlying truths within a dataset. ■ Create business intelligence reports.
Data Visualization	■ Organize open data thematically, well visualized, with logical application of metadata. ■ Use GIS platforms and other platforms to create spatial and temporal maps of policy issues to enhance insights.
Data Modeling, Engineering, and Data Science	■ Build and configure data infrastructure to facilitate analytics while ensuring accuracy, security, and reliability. ■ Clean and normalize large datasets. ■ Explore large datasets to look for patterns, trends, and insights. ■ Develop sophisticated models applying decision science and/ or machine learning to data problems. ■ Test models and refine based on test results. ■ Work with departments and other CDO staff to develop methods to operationalize models.
Performance Analysis	■ Provide predictive analytics support to stat programs.
Project Management	■ Establish management protocols and tools for data-driven projects.[a]

a. Jane Wiseman, "Lessons from Leading CDOs: A Framework for Better Civic Analytics," *Data-Smart City Solutions*, January 2017 (http://datasmart.ash.harvard.edu/news/article/lessons-from-leading-cdos-966).

the citywide data analytics center will, in turn, add better-trained data scientists who will take on larger, complicated systemic problems. "This is about the agencies owning the data and pushing it out, and eventually they are the ones, not me, that will create apps for the data," Coral says.

The Socio in the Socio-Technical Ecosystem

Technology is not the most critical component in unlocking the power of the new O/S. Integrated data and beautifully designed maps make the biggest difference when they spark the imagination of senior officials to ask the right questions. "What if we added more addiction counseling in the northwest part of our city—who would benefit and how would we measure success?" "If we wanted to help children get more exercise, what are the key drivers we can change to have an impact?"

This interaction of people and systems is an important component of the "socio" in the socio-technical ecosystem, and cities need to give this aspect as much attention as they do the technical part. Getting a bureaucracy that operates by routines to ask the right big questions is a lot more difficult than answering them, especially when the problem spans more than one department. "We urge our residents and public officials alike to simply *play* with the data. We do the hard work of putting it all in one place, but then you need to try different combinations," says Laura Meixell, assistant director of the Office of Innovation and Performance in Pittsburgh.

Playing with the data could mean combining property vacancies with criminal justice statistics to see where crimes drop or rise depending on the number of foreclosed buildings on a block or even, simply, what time of day crimes occur. Meixell notes, "Most people, including our own police officers, don't typically ask these questions. Well, now there are no more excuses."

Chris Brady and others, writing about how sports teams use data, make the case that organizations should incorporate data translators who can stimulate these questions and assist the program managers in understanding the potential of the "quants." The authors say translators need the following skills:

- Sufficient knowledge of the business to pass the "street cred" test with executive decisionmakers

- Sufficient analytics knowledge—or a willingness and ability to acquire it—to communicate effectively with the organization's data scientists

- The confidence to speak the truth to executives, peers, and subordinates

- A willingness to search for deeper knowledge about everything

- The drive to create both questions and answers in a form others find accessible

- An extremely high sense of quality standards and attention to detail

- The ability to engage at team or organizational meetings without being asked for input[6]

These data translators, regardless of their official titles, can assist the operating agencies in expediting important and necessary cultural changes in a new O/S, where the definition of performance for individuals, teams, and agencies will migrate from the measurement of activities to the measurement of outcomes. To get there, public officials will need to envision those questions, constantly challenging the quants to design analysis and reports that identify anomalies and new strategies.

The socio part of the new O/S also includes establishing and managing changes to how city departments handle hiring, communications, management, employee training, working in teams, solving problems, and other fundamental organizational responsibilities, as discussed throughout this book. The distributed system produces value through collaboration, for instance, and, thus, will need what Loo Geok Pee and Atreyi Kankanhalli say is the capacity "to develop strong capabilities in sharing, applying, and creating knowledge." To do so, they write, cities must retain intellectual capital, facilitate the training of new employees, and assist with the assimilation of innovative approaches.[7]

In addition to a Data Analytics Team responsible for creating a new set of standards, procedures, capacities, and relationships for each department's staff who handles data and technology City Hall needs to establish a Project Management Office (PMO) for the purposes of driving the organizational changes demanded by the new O/S. These modifications include instituting meaningful staff reorganization, analyzing and organizing work systems, researching and implementing legal compliance, and addressing human resources. The City Hall team would work with a project management official in each department who would handle these responsibilities that bridge to a new O/S.[8] Unlike the Data Analytics Team, the PMO will likely be assembled solely for the transition period—an ad hoc committee, perhaps augmented by outside consultants.

As with the Data Analytics Team, it is important that, regardless of its location or title, the city's PMO is backed by executive-level authority. The GeoHub in Los Angeles is an impressive program innovation and a clear example of the type of data-sharing hub this book recommends for distributed governance. However, to make the systemic, citywide changes required for a new O/S, City Hall cannot rely on voluntary acceptance of new norms, systems, and procedures. It must be able to require compliance by every department for both IT and operations.

One clear model for assembling a leadership organization that can move a city to distributed governance is this twin set of a Data Analytics Team and a PMO team, perhaps located in the Office of Management and Budget, each reporting to a high-level executive. This is not the only option. In Illinois, for instance, Bhatt as CIO handles day-to-day responsibilities of changing the state's data sharing protocols and associated tasks. In a full move to a new O/S, Illinois might want to keep that structure. Another government might want to merge the IT and operations support at City Hall instead of having two parallel offices. Local circumstances and strengths can dictate how City Hall builds its model; regardless, these responsibilities need a home.

PUBLIC SERVANTS IN THE DATA-INFUSED SYSTEM

Woe is the police officer, the public school teacher, and, yes, even the DMV agent. They are the public face of government, located at the point where policies get implemented, often bearing the brunt of citizens' frustration with how the city operates. Michael Lipsky spotlighted the importance of frontline staff in his groundbreaking work *Street-Level Bureaucracy*, published in 1980, where he deftly noted the many ways field-level workers affect policies by how they carry them out. Inevitably these public servants have choices in how they make decisions small and large, from whether to make an arrest to how far to take the "no smiling on your driver's license photo" rule. At the time, the prevailing public administration assumption was that street-level employees should follow rules, not exercise discretion.[9] Given the legacy of Tammany Hall-type corruption, it felt a bit dangerous to democratic norms to allow much variance in execution.

Recent technology breakthroughs have radically altered that formula. Now a well-designed system can explicitly grant discretion to street-level bureaucrats by equipping them with the information and training they need to make decisions that are not only as good as what the manual says but better, because those decisions match the circumstances at hand. And the system provides all of this while also furnishing the tools to ensure that this discretion is exercised properly.

The new O/S changes the life of the public servant in three important ways. It gives workers that authority in their day-to-day jobs to solve problems and address outliers. It facilitates improved access to high-level officials who are no longer shielded from good ideas by hierarchical bureaucracies. And it allows the workers to work sideways—providing a platform so an employee in one agency can more easily see other agencies' activities that connect to the location or policy questions he or she is focused on.

Vertical Structures: Worker Autonomy and Creativity

The socio-technical ecosystem supports many new capacities, but perhaps none more important than liberating workers from the command-and-control system and giving them the power to punch up through bureaucratic hierarchy. The existing system defines accountability as compliance, which undermines public worker motivation. As professors Thomas Schillemans and Madalina Busuioc note in their comprehensive work on this subject: "For motivated stewards, establishing one's reputation, realizing one's mission and achieving organizational goals is not logically connected to external scrutiny through accountability. To the contrary, tight controls and a lack of policy autonomy could actually 'crowd out' intrinsic motivation."[10]

The street-level bureaucrat benefits from how the new O/S automates routines, redirecting time from the mundane to activities that add value, while providing decision support tools to couple targeted analysis of powerful data with the worker's own hard-won experience. As with the child welfare workers in Alleghany County, public servants will receive information through an easy-to-use UX that gives them, in a single view, the information they need about the applicable address, or the circumstances of the student who has been sent to the principal's office, or the sewer system on the block where they are asked to solve a problem.

The underutilized day-to-day problem-solving ability of dedicated public employees provides a vast opportunity for new public value. Those who engage directly with the public—the retail work of cities—will always know more about the details of their jobs than their supervisors. An open system allows these public servants to implement these insights, providing digital documentation of the decisions they made rather than having to submit and then wait for permission to act. When a street crew sees that the block they are scheduled to pave does not need the asphalt but another area a block away does, they can deviate from their instructions if they photograph and document why they made that choice.

For perspective, let's apply these changes to a New York City police officer who would be using the NYPD Domain Awareness System (DAS) discussed in chapter 3. The assignment to the officer is crime reduction, which requires training, information, and community support. With the NYPD software advances, the cop receives highly customized information delivered to her smartphone. She receives texts from neighbors and is granted enhanced discretion concerning when an arrest makes sense. Performance for her depends on crime reduction and community respect, not just arrests. She can decide how to allocate her time among a range of activities that might make a difference in the neighborhood. This officer in the future will increasingly have more time for this valuable work as she experiences a dramatic reduction in her paperwork responsibilities, now handled by machines that would take her dispatches and dictation and quickly turn them into reports.

Top-Down Support for Bottom-Up Ideas

If street-level workers have the best insights about the work they do—and if a new level of autonomy is opening their minds to new ideas that they test on the job—it only makes sense that these ideas should be shared with City Hall for wider adoption. Quicker, flatter communication tools can leap over the barriers that have shielded managers and administrators from field ideas. Both culture and technology need to point in the same direction to facilitate this flow of ideas throughout the city workforce.

To consistently generate good ideas from employees, a city must create structures and programs that support such open communications. When Indianapolis set up a centralized unit dedicated to change management years ago, the city's innovation team assigned a person full-time to solicit and promote good ideas from the workforce. The team organized and facilitated email access from remote work sites, monthly meetings between labor leaders and the mayor, and a "job for a day" program where top leaders, including the mayor, worked in the field with employees.

Even before today's communications options, the results were impressive. Union workers explained how small changes in the sanitation trucks would increase productivity and decrease accidents. Others demonstrated how asphalt paving could be done with one fewer truck per crew by reconfiguring both the work teams and the mix of equipment. Employees explained how supervisor approvals of completed repairs in public housing—along with procurement problems that stymied getting the right part to the right place—slowed their response to tenant repair issues. When coupled with other structural reforms, new procedures based on ideas like these produced tens of millions of dollars in savings, qualitative service enhancements, and measurable improvements in the lives of workers in terms of increased compensation, better safety, and dramatically fewer grievances.

Digital idea platforms, email access straight to the top, contests and rewards for good ideas—these can all play a part in jumpstarting employee idea sharing, but they work much better with explicit support from the top. The mayor must clearly establish that supervisors need to support worker empowerment, backed up with top-line evaluation that reflects this priority. Without the assurance (and demand) that new ideas are welcome, supervisors will create an environment that stifles the free flow of worker information because they fear that recommendations for change somehow reflect badly on how they have operated their department to date. Innovation teams can play an important role in cultivating and driving transformative change, but they will produce even more success if they accept that part of their role is to promote the technology and culture that more broadly unlocks new value.

The city should also prime the pump of ideas by presenting open data in a way that is relevant to and accessible by staff with curation, data visualization, and presentation. Seeing a wider picture with more detail can spark all sorts of ideas. (Can you believe we have more vehicles than staff? Did you know that our parts room loses $100,000 a year in parts? Why are 45 percent of our parking tickets never collected?)

Gain Sharing for Employee Motivation

In chapter 1 we discussed how the Memphis Solid Waste Management Department faced a projected multi-million-dollar deficit brought on, in part, by an outmoded budget, personnel policies, pay, and internal services. In 2016 the department made substantial progress in solving those problems, thanks in large part to a vision that dates before WWII of how cities and their workers can work better together.

At the beginning of the Progressive era, Joe Scanlon, a labor leader in the steel industry, set out to create a better structure for management and labor. One of his proposals included gain sharing, which shares the savings from cost-cutting measures with the employees:

> What we are actually trying to say is simply this: That the average
> worker knows his own job better than anyone else, and that there

are a great many things that he could do if he has a complete understanding of the necessary. Given this opportunity of expressing his intelligence and ingenuity, he becomes a more useful and more valuable citizen in any given community or in any industrial operation.[11]

Not quite a century later then Memphis mayor A. C. Wharton directed the solid waste division to find a solution to the twin challenges of rising customer demands and budget deficits by implementing a labor-management partnership that used employee gain-sharing as a core strategy. The key to their efforts, according to Skip Stitt, an outside expert hired by the city, involved breaking through communication and information barriers. The workforce, managers, and the public all needed to be able to view how much it costs to repair garbage trucks, how much overtime is consumed, and what percentage of trash is recycled. Trusting field workers with more discretion means trusting them with more information about costs, service levels, and administrative overhead. That kind of information also helps the sanitation workers build stronger ideas for service improvements and cost savings.

According to Stitt, who has assisted with breakthroughs such as these across the country, success depends on "openness, transparency with information, ability to gather and share accurate data, candor, patience, willingness to spend time together working on issues and building trust, and a willingness to not just share the data but to share the gains as well."

A management-union team in Memphis began to focus on the annual $7.5 million expense line for the fleet services agency. Now able to see critical data, employees quickly identified that too many vehicles were kept in reserve and too many had annual repair costs of as much as $30,000 per year. They could see how often lack of preventive maintenance drove up total costs. They also reviewed routes and procedures for garbage pickup. Over eighteen months, with the ongoing support of newly elected mayor Jim Strickland and AFSCME Local 1733, which also brought in a consultant for the process, the Solid Waste Management

Department developed and implemented an Improvement Plan that addressed the issues.

Because of the operational improvements that were implemented, the Solid Waste Fund saved $166,941 in its first fiscal year, 80 percent of which was distributed to the department's full-time, nonmanagement employees. Memphis saw continued meaningful performance improvements, including a 17 percent drop in customer service complaints from June to October 2016 and a monthly all-time high in collected recycling volume.

What Scanlon envisioned and Memphis enacted should now be routine and continuous in city departments across the country. In Memphis, no one lost his job due to a need for the department to get more efficient. Productivity produces better service levels, and so the number of jobs can be rationalized as workers retire.

The Horizontal Structure: The Interagency Hub

Interagency cooperation does not come easily. Everything about city government reinforces silos. Agencies use distinct software and manage performance almost entirely on agency-focused metrics. The reputation of, and accolades for, staff is determined by how well they perform agency-assigned tasks. Successful participation in cross-agency teams rarely has the same professional effect.

However, the more systemic and complex the problem, the more agencies need to integrate ideas and resources. Take the construction of the Second Avenue subway line in New York City. During construction, the Metropolitan Transit Agency (MTA) focused on the complex, massive task of building the tunnels and stations, while other agencies worked around them. Sanitation workers struggled to find places on the street where they could stop their trucks to pick up resident trashcans and not block traffic. Sanitation inspectors gave citations to shop owners for trash in front of their stores, and the owners were incensed because most of the debris was from the city's own MTA construction crews. Traffic cops handed out parking tickets to delivery trucks forced to double-park to unload.

For two years no one pulled the agencies into one room to look more comprehensively at the effect of disruption on neighbors and shop owners until Lolita Jackson, an enterprising young woman in one of the city agencies, found the ear of the deputy mayor with an idea for how to get the agencies to work together. That team, in conjunction with the people working and living in the construction area, created temporary procedures near the construction site. The result: better signage for retailers, redesigned trash receptacles and trash pickup routes, and a quick-stop parking zone for delivery trucks.[12]

Cities are faced with many issues that aren't within the jurisdiction of just one agency, and most are even more vexing than angry store-owners near the Second Avenue subway. Affordable housing helps families avoid eviction, which means the children don't have to change schools, which improves their educational outcomes, which makes them more likely to find a well-paying job when they become adults. When a stretch of riverfront is ready for some new activity, what gets priority? Industry, apartments, parks, roads? Would mixed-use development be best at that site—and if so, who should be talking together to make that a reality? Cross-functional teams play an important part in governance, and a robust body of literature exists on how to support and manage them, but officials cannot set up a taskforce each time a person in one agency needs to coordinate or brainstorm with another.

Prior to the breakthrough technologies of the five years, leading academics Elinor and Vincent Ostrom over decades studied these spatially organized networks and their complex multidimensional problems. Carina Wyborn of the Luc Hoffman Institute summarizes their work, noting that "adaptive governance scholarship focuses on institutional design and cross-scale institutional linkages through nested and polycentric approaches to collaborative governance."[13] Today's tools provide a partial solution to this complexity.

The new O/S makes sharing horizontal, inter-agency information much easier. The GeoHub in Los Angeles, for example, provides high-quality visualization tools on a sophisticated cloud-powered platform, allowing data to be organized by address. In distributed governance, when most city documents, reports, photos, and inspections are geo-tagged, the resulting easy access will produce more everyday cross-agency insights. The new platform should sharply reduce the time associated with finding out what other facilities or programs are occurring in the same community—or are planned to be soon. In a few years, AI could even contact a city worker with suggestions for documents, studies, and permits related to a project but hidden away in digital file cabinets throughout the government.

In some cases workers may need to create a more intentional network, whether as a place to share thoughts with others working in the community or as part of a more structured team where these virtual connections "will need to evolve into learning platforms along with the stronger collaborative relationship."[14] Professor Amy Edmondson of the Harvard Business School, a leading expert in the study of teams, describes the need for "figurative scaffolding" or a "light, temporary structure that supports the process of construction."[15] Although she conceives of this scaffolding as support for teams that meet and need organized help to produce action, the concept could also include geo-tagged learning platforms. This scaffolding will reduce the transactional friction and cost of being on a team, making it easier to collaborate without the time and complexity of forming a taskforce.

The GeoHub also provides a glimpse of how figurative scaffolding can work in the new O/S. For Los Angeles' participation in the international effort to reduce pedestrian injuries, called Vision Zero, the GeoHub's group feature built with ESRI enabled city and county users to share data that created a High Injury Network, a story map exploring streets with a high concentration of traffic collisions. Spurred by ideas from accessing data from departments across City Hall—and newly established relationships fostered by Coral's team—more cross-agency work is happening, as well. For example, the Bureau of Engineering, Bureau of Street Services, and the Department of Transportation have worked together to create shared maps to better coordinate efforts on large capital projects—in a sense, the easy-to-use maps have fostered collaboration that should have happened long before. According to Coral:

> We're seeing a lot of sub-groups emerge from different agencies. Remember agencies don't tend to steer towards collaboration, so data might be what gets them to collaborate on their own

volition. This is not me pushing over and over. This is them now knowing they can use the Hub; they realize they don't need us to help them, the tools are so easy to use and the data is so intuitive.

Amen Mashariki, the former chief analytics officer for New York City, took L.A.'s GeoHub to the next generation of enhancements, in what he dubbed the "Citywide Intelligence Hub." The Intelligence Hub allows users to share data with each other through a user interface oriented around geographic tools and pairs sophisticated GIS analytics with easy-to-use mapping tools, which provides broad-based functionality throughout different departments and from executive-level decisionmakers to the field-level operational user. Highly trained scientists in the mayor's Office of Data Analytics can also analyze the data for more complex assignments. In 2016 NYC strengthened the GIS virtual scaffolding that supported cross-agency collaboration through real scenario data drills, the first of which involved emergency management, by building relationships and identifying what data could be easily found on the Intelligence Hub and what could not be found or used.

Encouraging and Protecting Risk Takers

Almost anything out of the ordinary in the daily life of a public employee involves risk. Mechanically abiding by the rules that control the status quo is the safest path. The largest obstacle in the way of a pivot to problem-solving public employees is not how tech-savvy they might be but, rather, their appetite for risk. The public employee who sees risk in change or altering a procedure to produce better results is acting totally rationally. The action may not be appreciated by peers, probably is not favored by supervisors, runs the risk of a second-guess by auditors or inspectors general, and, of course, the ultimate career killer, an angry media story.

Therefore one of the most important implementation steps to the new O/S is for municipal leadership to rebalance the risk/reward ratio. Elected officials and agency leaders can apply their thumbs to the scale in the following ways:

- Publicly set the goals and outcomes and then relentlessly manage them. A mayor cannot state his goals and then, behind the scenes, manage for political or other reasons, demanding, for example, literacy targets for all students and then protecting an after-school reading program run by a politically connected organization that shows awful results in terms of outcomes.

- Reward high performers and risk takers with recognition, promotion, more responsibility, and/or bonuses or other financial compensation.

- Protect those who make well-intentioned and honest mistakes; give them a safe harbor to fail. This can include defending good people when they make mistakes or take the blame oneself as their leader. Not being thrown under the bus breeds enormous loyalty and cultivates a willingness to take risks.

- Get out in front and show others you are personally willing to take risks. A mayor or department head cannot expect staff to take risks when the boss is clearly avoiding risk, protecting himself or herself, or blaming others.

- Make sure performance scorecards reflect outcomes not only by agency but also among peers (for example, how does the NW quadrant of the street department fare around public satisfaction and smooth streets when compared to the SW quadrant).

- Create digital tools that allow the field worker to show that her decision was guided by evidence so that, if second-guessed, she has documented support.

- Create a public dialog more intolerant of a mediocre status quo.

MANAGING MORE AUTONOMOUS EMPLOYEES

Employees' job descriptions and relationships profoundly change in the new O/S, and management needs to change, as well. Instead of waiting for a problem to occur and then dealing with it—or reading case files looking for the needle-in-the-haystack problem—supervisors now need to manage by the numbers. The engaged street-level bureaucrat may not require so many layers of compliance-oriented supervisors, but he still needs training and, in some instances, discipline. As Eric Welch and Sanjay Pandey correctly point out, "the rule-bound character of public organizations persists both as an important means of ensuring accountability and responsiveness and as a potentially pernicious constraint on efficient operation, coordination, communication, managerial initiative, and innovativeness."[16]

In the new O/S, managers need to be able to determine how lower-level employees use their discretion and ensure that these workers produce results and follow appropriate rules and norms. Democratic governance requires that employees act fairly and without bias or favoritism. The corollary of more street-level discretion is better management insight concerning how those employees make decisions. This new form of accountability that better balances compliance and discretion includes three components that can be measured:

- **Outcomes:** Did children in need of services who were removed from their homes do better? Were there fewer health and safety problems in restaurants or building sites that have been inspected?

- **Individual or team performance:** How did this employee or team perform compared to peers in terms of outputs? Do they meet or exceed well-researched benchmarks?

- **Fairness:** What does the data reflect concerning whether an employee fairly applies the laws regardless of the background or ethnicity of the person involved?

Whether evaluating outcomes or insuring fairness by employees in their treatment of citizens or determining how one person in an agency supports or works with another, the technical power of a new O/S can provide massively more insights, which, in turn, will facilitate responsiveness. Cases can be evaluated against a range of metrics and the results easily displayed on dynamic dashboards. Managers can see the outliers in terms of good and deficient performance, aided with machine grading of case notes that suggest to the supervisor whether a certain group of employees has a high percentage of cases missing information, or whether the same phrase is repeatedly used to describe interactions with different persons (indicating a rote or copied response).

Democratic governance requires that supervisors look not just at outcomes but also at these higher-level objectives of legality, equity, and ethics. The new O/S can help managers determine if members of their team acted fairly and in the best interest of the public. That same machine grading, for instance, can use sentiment analysis to see if an employee is displaying attitudes about certain populations.

One of the most important pivots involves using data to identify employees who need help, before a serious incident occurs rather than after. The data science team at the University of Chicago worked with the Charlotte-Mecklenburg Police Department to identify police officers at risk for involvement in an "adverse interaction with a member of the public."[17] The Chicago researchers' goal was to help supervisors "more accurately target training, counseling, and other interventions toward officers who are at highest risk of having an adverse incident" and reduce the time and administrative overhead spent working with officers not at risk.[18]

The approach, which could be applied to many other government situations, involves looking at data in more than a dozen different areas, including internal affairs, dispatch events, citations, traffic stops, arrests, employee records, and training. The information included officers who received conduct violations or counseling, had preventable accidents, the number of domestic violence runs, and more. The analysts found situational factors and characteristics that are predictive of adverse events and devised a model that increased positive identification by 10 percent to 20 percent and decreased false positives by 30 percent to 50 percent. Information predicting that an officer may respond in a tense situation differently than his peers allows the command staff and supporting services to offer assistance to the officer. Using data to reduce the number of unnecessary confrontations between police and residents by preemptively dealing with officers most likely to go beyond correct protocol will enhance the legitimacy of the police and of the city government itself, as well.

Of course no one tool is a panacea. As the authors of the report describe, even with these data-driven insights officials still need to deal with "the complex web of cognitive, interactional, social, and institutional factors affecting the relationship between the police and the public."[19] In addition, when using data science it is critical to guard against bias. Harry Surden, a scholar at University of Colorado Law School, points out that "although sometimes the embedding of values [in artificial intelligence-driven technological systems] is intentional, often it is unintentional and, in either case, when it occurs it can be difficult to observe or detect."[20]

When a predictive model "trains" on data that includes bias, the model can perpetuate that bias.[21] This potential problem does not lessen the utility of prediction if policymakers guiding the science think rigorously about the underlying assumptions. In fact, a positive result can occur when that process uncovers a bias and then moves to remedy it.

NEW O/S FOR HUMAN RESOURCES

The administrative structure of cities today—how they hire and acquire, in particular—focuses much more on policing compliance than on finding and preparing the right employees and equipping them with the correct tools. Modernizing City Hall requires new approaches to the basic administrative systems. City officials certainly have the technical capacity to more accurately help them find, train, and employ the best individuals by building data-driven systems that identify the characteristics of high-performing employees. Yet today it is essentially illegal to hire based on quality or to promote based on results.

Twenty-First-Century Hiring

Cities labor under obsolete hiring procedures. Because of legal prohibitions and decades of precedent, grievances, and lawsuits, many older municipalities still operate processes that generate ranked lists of employees based on tests that are not always germane, sometimes known as the rule of three. The three highest scores go to the department doing the hiring, although that process may not even produce the talents needed on the job. New York City still annually administers 1,000 civil service tests to place people in jobs. Delays are caused by long lead times, lots of hierarchy, and centralized decisionmaking about who makes it to the shortlist, which almost guarantee that many of the best candidates are no longer available at the end.

The cumbersome and often irrelevant hiring process used today in most cities is particularly galling because it is a hurdle in the way of finding the workforce that can get the most from the new O/S. Public officials who excel at negotiation, team building, collaboration, and contract management will be necessary, and government will need many more tech savvy employees. But as the consulting firm McKinsey predicts, "there will be a shortage of talent necessary for organizations to take advantage of big data. By 2018, the United States alone could face a shortage of 140,000 to 190,000 people with deep analytical skills, as well as 1.5 million managers and analysts with the know-how to use the analysis of big data to make effective decisions."[22]

The people most needed for a data-driven culture are the very ones least likely to put up with long, irrelevant procedures. Millennials don't want narrow jobs and constrained authority. For a city to recruit the entrepreneurial workers that are attracted to and will perform well in distributed governance, it must recognize that the old model of specialized, tenure-based employment is of limited appeal. Where vacancies call for technical skills already in demand in the private sector, the problem becomes even more extreme.

A modernized approach would use data to project vacancies, allowing positions to be filled before employees retire, thus avoiding both the loss of knowledge and sometimes unnecessary overtime resulting from a vacancy. Let HR use its data to project the characteristics of employees who do the best job at the position and who don't leave too quickly. Allowing high-performing department heads more authority to directly hire with much less central HR oversight can make a difference, as well.

Government efficiency experts Katherine Barrett and Richard Greene, writing in *Governing Magazine* last year under the all-too-true title "Can Government Hiring Get Out of the Stone Age?,"[23] underscored changes in Kansas that gave agencies the authority to hire some people as unclassified—that is, not subject to civil service rules. In agencies that are taking advantage of aspects of the new law, employees can elect to forgo civil service protection, often in exchange for a potential increase in pay or a change in job duties. Of course procedures need to be in place to make sure that a more flexible system does not even inadvertently discriminate against minority workers. Plenty of lawsuits across the country against cities have shown what an MIT research paper described as "a cautionary lesson for employers with merit-based approaches for attracting, selecting, and retaining their best employees: If not implemented carefully, such efforts can trigger demographic biases."[24]

Public sector employers compete for talent with the nonprofit and for-profit sectors. In a post-patronage environment, hiring the best available applicant requires new techniques and speed. A promise to "get back to you within nine months," or whatever the city average might be, just won't work. In one area government does possess a differentiating edge over the private sector—mission. Many young millennials want to contribute by having a sense of purpose about their work. Even with the challenges of pay, a public service interest will attract individuals if they believe they can make a difference—which the modernized infrastructure should allow. A Deloitte survey found that nine out of ten millennials want to work in a business "measured by something more than just its financial success."[25] Advancing the centrality of producing public value will help the recruiting effort.

Bob Lavigna and John Flato, writing in a blog about recruiting intelligence, take on the cause of how the public sector can effectively compete for talent by concentrating on university recruiting and partnerships.[26] Their suggestions, already occurring in small pilots across the United States, include establishing deep relationships with schools that might assign interns or fellows to augment the city workforce. In these cases, though, the city needs to fast track opportunities for the interns to receive permanent jobs. According to Lavigna, the Federal Office of Personnel

Management's new Pathways program has made it easier to hire interns into permanent (full-time) jobs by creating a special hiring track for those who excel.

To be clear, these issues are not solely for hiring data analysts and other white-collar employees. In the new O/S, cities need workers in all positions who are capable, committed, and able to work semi-autonomously, from police officers to teachers to park district maintenance. Hiring procedures by the city and assumptions about what it's like to work for the city by jobseekers (which clearly can be based on fact in some of today's systems) are limiting the ability of municipal departments to build the workforce they need to succeed.

More Effective Training

New rules and opportunities for employees mean new training to get them ready, willing, and able. For instance, child abuse expert William Simon led a study in 2009 with child health policy expert Kathleen Noonan, looking at how accountability in child welfare systems could be adapted to balance "programmatic flexibility" and legal mandates. In one track, workers in Utah and Alabama were guided through a step-by-step training process for rules and compliance of how to handle cases from start to end. Training in the other track, a reform model, focused more on skills such as interviewing, planning, and teaming well with other agencies, giving the trainees the ability to adapt and react to different situations. The authors reported impressionistic evidence that the latter model resulted in dramatic improvement.[27]

Remarkably little research exists on how public-sector training programs produce better results. Yet equipping bureaucrats with data tools and authorizing them to make decisions that will drive outcomes will not suffice without training. Cities will need to establish training that is more complex and rigorous than what has been provided to date for simple rule compliance.

A massive need in training for a new O/S is a focus on professional development to engender employees' interest in data skills and problem-solving. Many of the better tech vendors lament that the products purchased by government allow much more functionality than employees utilize. Dramatic improvement in labor productivity requires better and broader training to produce a data-savvy workforce. Public officials need to know enough about the capabilities of easy-to-use cloud software to be able to regularly ask those what-if questions discussed earlier in this chapter.

Denver is setting the pace with its establishment of a workforce program called Peak Academy, which sends nearly every administrator through a three-day set of workshops on creative problem-solving.[28] City employees benefit both from the curriculum itself and from the encouragement they receive simply for exercising discretion and positing new efficiencies, including mayoral recognition of top ideas and agency-wide web postings. Louisville and many other cities have instituted similar internal training academies based on Six Sigma or other performance management regimens.

Joy Bonaguro, the energetic chief data officer of the city and county of San Francisco, has taken a national lead in training city employees. Her shop, in partnership with the City Controller, offers well-attended classes in a range of services at the Data Academy, a collection of tool- and skill-focused workshops designed for San Francisco employees. Started in early 2014 Data Academy has grown from two courses to more than thirteen, and the number of students/employees has also grown from eighty trained in the first year to more than 600 in FY2016 and over 700 in FY2017.[29]

The training academy grew, in part, from free micro-workshops on Tableau data visualization offered by the controller's office developed to introduce city employees to the power of visualized data in a way that did not take them away from their jobs for long. Now the Data Academy trainings are in two- to three-hour segments, with priorities driven by user requests. Topics have included data usability, information design, business process mapping, and a "train the trainer" model to teach key personnel in departments with high demand for specific courses to become teachers themselves.

"Students feel that Data Academy removes the intimidation factor of new programs and gives them enduring reference materials. Students experience 'aha' moments when they are exposed to a new way of thinking about data. This is at the heart of what Data Academy hopes to achieve," says Blake Valenta, a data fellow in the city's data shop. He points to the Ethics Commission, whose staff members were early attendees of the Tableau course, became excited about the power of visualization, and went on to use database-locked data about campaign finance to create dashboards easily accessible to the public.

According to Sam Abbott, a controller analyst working on Data Academy, these efforts helped create a universal language of data, which, in turn, produced new ways of thinking about problems and solutions.[30] These empowering tools change the way public employees think and, in turn, enhance their responsiveness. A recent three-month survey by the controller's office revealed an estimated $1.7 million in annual savings for the city, and an average savings of 1.4 hours a week per person due to skills acquired at Data Academy.[31]

There is also a need for even more advanced training that individual cities cannot address on their own. Academic institutions, particularly public policy and administration schools, should start preparing current and future public servants to deploy advanced data skills. This means offering coursework that moves far beyond traditional statistical methods. Government agencies need at least some employees who are ready to take on more complex data challenges. To do that they need to know how to use tools like R and Python to link the vast spectrum of administrative datasets enmeshed within splintered agencies and to understand both the advantages and the perils of machine learning techniques.

One encouraging model is the Applied Data Analytics program established through a partnership between New York University, the University of Chicago, and the University of Maryland. With funding from the U.S. Census Bureau and the Arnold Foundation, the program takes a very different approach to standard public administration programs. A set textbook and curriculum cover core areas of big data management and analysis, but it is the students (government employees at the local and federal level) who bring real-world challenges to the class. Participants are broken into teams and must develop data-driven approaches to solving these problems. This approach both engages the students in the curriculum and ensures that they leave with practical skills and policy solutions that can be brought back to their home agency.

More Efficient Procurement

No existing municipal administrative area produces more drag on in-novation than procurement, where employees, haunted by the thought that some media outlet will accuse them of favoritism or insufficient attention to an arcane process detail, follow those processes to the letter, even in circumstances when they are far from applicable or even logical. A procurement system that promotes support to the public service worker rather than simple compliance as its goal will unlock vast value.

This section is not a step-by-step guide to how to reform procure-ment, but it does outline some ways in which the new O/S platform can support distributed learnings and reform around the issue. A vast aca-demic and consultant literature exists on procurement that we do not cover in this book.[32] These few principles concern how better use of open data will improve the ways procurement can support newly em-powered employees.

Connect the users of purchased items to those who procure. Pro-curement officials do not listen closely enough to their users, missing the chance to incorporate the knowledge of the employees who order and subsequently rely on the equipment, materials, and tools. When pro-curement is integrated with program management, open governance will allow a continuing conversation before and after the procurement process, including insights from those who are administering the pro-gram or using the equipment.

Loosen compliance details in return for more transparency. Strict, agonizingly long adherence to every imaginable procurement detail does not produce value. Long processes distort procurement. In one in-stance for a major procurement in a large city the procurement lawyers would not let the department listen to its own advisor's insights because of a worry that the city could be accused of not strictly adhering to a numerically driven process. The new O/S can power transparency, speed, and flexibility without sacrificing integrity.

Connect the IoT sensors to better lifecycle management and ac-quisition. Asset procurement today often is not matched well against lifecycle costing; for example, exactly when does a bridge need repair or a garbage truck need to be retired? Open governance will incorporate the sensor information from bridge vibrations or from city truck or car engines to assist in identifying exactly when to procure or schedule repairs.

Value speed and modularity in IT procurement. The procedures for purchasing government software were developed from practices ten to twenty years ago, when the city would purchase a large enterprise software system and then add an often separate RFP for expensive integration services to help with the installation. In these circumstances, the procurement and installation took an excessive amount of time and the bidders were evaluated on a set of tight deliverables for a sturdy, stable, and, for the most part, static system. New IT improvements for cities today continue to roll out in micro-cloud-like offerings. As the rate of IT changes accelerates, the old procurement model of highly prescriptive RFPs with long lead times is increasingly unnecessary and obsolete. Procurement shops need to purchase more quickly, in smaller chunks, on an as-needed business, and as a service. According to the specialized federal government digital shop 18F, procurement officials will be able to reduce risk and deliver more quickly with modular contracting that breaks up complex IT software and app procurements "into multiple, tightly-scoped projects."[33]

Chapter 5 **THE BOTTOM LINE**

Key Points

- City administrative systems are more driven by an ethos of compliance than one of finding and preparing the right employees and providing them the tools needed to improve programs and services.

- New technologies and access to far more datasets can transform rule-bound workers into street-level problem-solvers. Bold experiments in Los Angeles and Allegheny County have shown that, with the right distributive data platform, agencies can collaborate and build faster and more responsive services.

- Leadership is essential to advance a new O/S and is comprised of three significant steps:

- Executive Leadership: The very top elected/appointed official must articulate a commitment to O/S principles and assign a chief with cross-agency authority to operationalize the transition.

- O/S Elements: The new O/S must be supported by a clear vision, engagement, and operations strategy. This should include a significant number of operational specifics, such as contained in the Equipt to Innovate framework.

- Data Analytics Team and Project Management Office: Central responsibility must be established to encourage, organize, and support the development of a new O/S throughout the enterprise.

Pitfalls

- Although key executive leaders will provide clear directives and rules for participants, a new O/S is not a centralized system. The need for central support for an open, distributed system should not be mistaken as a top-down system.

- Discretion for frontline workers must be balanced with more outcome-based supervision at the senior level, utilizing much more data to discern which employees are excelling or should be better trained or redeployed.

Recommendations

- Embrace labor. Management and labor can collaborate when both benefit from O/S reforms that provide greater savings and efficiencies.

- There is no need for all municipal staff to become equally data-savvy, but they must be prepared to ask the right questions. With distributed data coming from many sources, government officials and frontline workers need to focus on clarifying what they want to know.

- Reforming hiring practices will be necessary in the long run to attract the right talent to government, and new training academies can inculcate core O/S principles and data skills that can help move the existing workforce toward more autonomy.

Examples

▪ Allegheny County's data warehouse has equipped caseworkers with comprehensive and real-time data about the families they are charged with assisting. The warehouse was built by "working around" traditional government systems: using foundation grants for initial R&D and establishing an outside HR pipeline attracting top tech talent from local universities.

▪ The Los Angeles GeoHub embodies distributive government as a central geo-coded open data portal that has made data far more accessible for agencies and citizens alike, fostering inter-agency collaborations.

NOTES

1. Donald F. Kettl, *Escaping Jurassic Government: Restoring America's Lost Commitment to Competence* (Brookings Institution Press, 2016), p. 155.

2. Majida Mehana and Arthur J. Reynolds, "School Mobility and Achievement: A Meta-analysis," *Children and Youth Service Review* 26 (2004), pp. 93–119.

3. J. Ramon Gil-Garcia, "Toward a Smart State? Inter-Agency Collaboration, Information Integration, and Beyond," *Information Polity* 17 (2012), p. 270.

4. Ibid.

5. See Equipt to Innovate, "Key Outcome Elements" (http://www.govern ing.com/equipt/about-the-equipt-framework.html#About+the+Equipt+Frame work).

6. Chris Brady, Mike Forde, and Simon Chadwick, "Why Your Company Needs Data Translators," *Harvard Business Review* (Winter 2017).

7. Loo Geok Pee and Atreyi Kankanhalli, "Interaction Among Factors Influencing Knowledge Management in Public-Sector Organizations: A Resource-Based View," *Government Information Quarterly* 33 (January 2016), p. 3.

8. See Howard Risher, "How to Maximize Employee Performance," *Government Executive*, May 2, 2017 (www.govexec.com/excellence/promising -practices/2017/05/how-maximize-employee-performance/137354).

9. Michael Lipsky, *Street-Level Bureaucracy* (New York: Russell Sage Foundation, 1980).

10. Thomas Schillemans and Madalina Busuioc, "Predicting Public Sector Accountability," *Journal of Public Administration Research and Theory* 25 (January 2015), p. 209.

11. Joe Scanlon quoted in "Why Scanlon Matters: Understanding Epic Leadership Principles," by Paul Davis and Larry Spears, Scanlon Foundation (2009), p. 7.

12. Stephen Goldsmith and Susan Crawford, *The Responsive City: Engaging Communities through Data-Smart Governance* (San Francisco: Jossey-Bass, 2014), pp. 95–96.

13. Carina Wyborn, "Cross-Scale Linkages in Connectivity Conservation: Adaptive Governance Challenges in Spatially Distributed Networks," *Environmental Policy and Governance*, July 21, 2014.

14. Ora-orn Poocharoen and Norma H. Wong, "Performance Management of Collaborative Projects: The Stronger the Collaboration, the Less is Measured," *Governance, Organization Public Performance and Management Review* 39 (March 2016), p. 607.

15. Amy C. Edmondson, "Teamwork on the Fly," *Harvard Business Review* (April 2012), p. 6.

16. Eric Welch and Sanjay Pandey, "E-Government and Bureaucracy: Toward a Better Understanding of Intranet Implementation and Its Effect on Red Tape," *Journal of Public Administration Research and Theory* 17 (July 2007), p. 379.

17. Samuel Carton and others, "Identifying Police Officers at Risk of Adverse Events," *Proceedings of the 22nd ACM SIGKDD International Conference on Knowledge Discovery and Data Mining* (August 2016), p. 9.

18. Ibid.

19. Ibid., p. 10.

20. Harry Surden, "Values Embedded in Legal Artificial Intelligence" (University of Colorado Law School, March 13, 2017).

21. Nikhil Sonnad, "Data Scientist Cathy O'Neil on the Cold Destructiveness of Big Data," *Quartz* (December 7, 2016) (https://qz.com/819245/data-scientist-cathy-oneil-on-the-cold-destructiveness-of-big-data).

22. James Manyika and others, "Big Data: The Next Frontier for Innovation, Competition, and Productivity," *McKinsey and Company* (www.mckinsey.com/business-functions/digital-mckinsey/our-insights/big-data-the-next-frontier-for-innovation).

23. Katherine Barrett and Richard Greene, "Can Government Hiring Get Out of the Stone Age?," *Governing*, February 2016 (www.governing.com/topics/mgmt/gov-government-hiring-best-practices.html).

24. Emilio J. Castilla, "Achieving Meritocracy in the Workplace," *MIT Sloan: Management Review* (Summer 2016).

25. Deloitte, "The 2017 Deloitte Millennial Survey," 2017 (www2.deloitte .com/global/en/pages/about-deloitte/articles/millennialsurvey.html), p. 11.

26. Bob Lavigna and John Flato, "Recruiting Against the Private Sector: What Government Can Do to Better to Compete for Talent From Campus," *Ere*, April 2, 2014 (www.eremedia.com/ere/recruiting-against-the-private-sector-what -government-can-do-to-better-to-compete-for-talent-from-campus).

27. Kathleen G. Noonan and others, "Legal Accountability in the Service-Based Welfare State: Lessons from Child Welfare Reform," *Law of Social Inquiry* 34, no. 3, 2009.

28. Brian Elms and J. B. Wogan, *Peak Performance: How Denver's Peak Academy Is Saving Money, Boosting Morale and Just Maybe Changing the World*, (Washington, D.C.: Governing, 2016).

29. Blake Valenta, "San-Francisco's Data Academy Develops a Data-Savvy Workforce," *Data-Smart City Solutions*, February 2017 (http://datasmart.ash .harvard.edu/news/article/san-franciscos-data-academy-develops-a-data-savvy -workforce-973).

30. Ibid.

31. Sam Abbott and others, "The Results Are in: Data Academy Makes a Big Impact!," *DataSF*, June 26, 2017 (https://datasf.org/blog/the-results-are-in -data-academy-makes-a-big-impact).

32. Deloitte, *Economic Benefits of Better Procurement Practices*, 2015 (www2 .deloitte.com/content/dam/Deloitte/au/Documents/Economics/deloitte-au-the -procurement-balancing-act-170215.pdf).

33. See General Services Administration: 18F, "Modular Contracting" (https:// modularcontracting.18f.gov).

SIX

Mashed Up Government

It seems quite simple and seamless. You click a button on Amazon and an article of clothing appears at your house. Behind the friction-free experience, however, is a highly complex system built on a savvy mix of data and coordination of many different organizations. A vendor used analytics to decide which items to offer to customers and where and how to digitally display them. Amazon created an online shopping experience customized for you, built with information from diverse sources about your specific needs and priorities. Other shoppers shared their opinions about the product on a platform designed to aid your final decision. UPS, after it received the shipping request from Amazon, used its mapping and logistics software to configure the most efficient delivery route to your house, which it conveyed to the driver on his mobile device. A third-party payment platform handled the credit card information, and the credit card company then divided your payment between Amazon and the vendor.

The many pieces of this highly distributed system are held together by data organized to produce a keen understanding of, and great experience for, the customer. The greater the knowledge, the better the decisions.

So why would anyone settle for the old days, when shopping took so much more time and when information was so much more limited?

Contrast this retail experience to how relatively little information municipal leaders have at their fingertips when making decisions and furnishing services. The citizens who are the ostensible customers are almost never consulted about what they want, when they want it, or how it will be delivered. Then again, neither are other city agencies that often have a perspective on the issue, nor experts such as professors at local universities who study the issue, and best practices. City government isn't making plans and programs in a pitch-black room, but it's awfully dark in there.

Consider, for example, the goal of helping a young man who has become enmeshed in the criminal justice system move into a more productive life trajectory. In today's system, does he, his family, or the authorities making the decision of where he will receive social services have access to ratings by other individuals in similar circumstances about the third-party nonprofits who offer the programs? Or can they access data about the programs' success as determined by recidivism, educational, or employment outcomes? When the judge is considering referral to treatment in lieu of detention, can he or she get comprehensive information about the young adult involved—any school problems, learning disabilities, or family history? Can the probation officer working for the judge on placement for the young man find the success rate of the agency under consideration as it relates to similar individuals?

In the big picture, public sector environments such as the criminal justice system share common elements with the retail one: delivering a crucial product or service to a person who needs it. These systems are every bit as fragmented and even more complex than the one Amazon runs, yet with much greater consequences and substantially less data integration or analysis.

In the new O/S, the city's role moves from owning data to gathering, curating, and coding it; from running an ad hoc and ill-informed system to overseeing a well-organized service network. Chapter 5 explored how cities can build a socio-technical ecosystem that gathers and uses data to empower their own departments and workers in that network, giving them far more information and far more autonomy.

This chapter is about third-party governance—the improvements that can be created by integrating the efforts of people who aren't on the city payroll and organizations that aren't part of city government. By turning outward, the knowledge base of a city vastly expands from a limited, small set of metrics, mining and weaving together information from third parties, sensors in IoT networks, social media, resident information submitted by smartphone photos, and the products of machine-read documents.

This distributed system also uses that new collective knowledge to activate partners outside of government. In some respects, this notion builds on the theory of "network government" articulated in 2007 by Goldsmith and Eggers in *Governing by Network,* which explained how best to manage the delivery of public services through networks of public, nonprofit, and private providers.[1] In that model, government creates and leads intentional networks that include other parties to deliver a specific service, such as operating a park or combating joblessness. The role of the public sector changes in the distributed system to a more intangible one, organized less around the delivery of a service and more about setting roles and rules for conduct, quality, equity, and privacy. As stated by Jeremy Millard, "although government should mobilize its own resources and talent better, there is always more relevant talent outside any organization (including government) than inside."[2]

Taken together, the distributed system's mix of information and actions from within and outside of city government is the very definition of doing more with more: more outreach to communities, residents, and partners like universities and local foundations, leading to more effective services that reach more individuals more responsively and with more legitimacy in how the services are delivered. Trust evolves from understanding and responsiveness. A traditional, closed, hierarchical City Hall appears indifferent to the needs and ideas of those it serves. The old truism holds: people won't care how much you know until they know how much you care. By setting up a new system, both literally and figuratively, cities establish transparency, listen to community suggestions, and respond more quickly. That demonstrates concern, which in the end creates trust.

DATA CONFIGURED FOR KANSAS CITY'S CITIZENS

Embracing an innovative approach to governing, let alone creating a whole new operating system, is hard for any public organization to pull off. But Kansas City, Missouri, has gone further than most. The city set in motion a new orientation and culture of data-informed government that shifted funding and citywide priorities, due, in large part, to how the changes consistently engage citizens with elected and appointed officials. Kansas City provides one model of how cities can organize their processes in a way that supports and encourages distributed governance.

It all began with significant turnover in local government. The 2011 election brought both a new mayor to the city, Sly James, as well as several new council members. The officials took advantage of the moment to do something seemingly banal: working together to develop a five-year, citywide business plan as a way to end the city's recent history of charting a municipal course with year-by-year budgets with virtually no revenue growth. They reasoned that any long-range planning must be done with citizen input.

This twin focus on planning and citizen input led to a complete revision of the city's policymaking and revenue allocation. The linchpin to the innovative approach was a longstanding quarterly community survey, coupled with citizen focus groups. Some cities engage in this kind of survey, but most do not work to integrate the responses into their strategic planning processes. Kansas City spent time getting it right, tailoring questions so they aligned with agency services and directly addressed citizen concerns. The city could depend on the responses it received since they represented almost a 50 percent response rate from the 9,000 distributed surveys.

This process led to new priorities and funding decisions. Citizens made it clear they would like a focus on community and neighborhood development, including issues like addressing local blight from the city's large inventory of abandoned structures. Each year, the city would knock down some buildings, but barely enough to keep up with newly derelict buildings, leaving virtually no improvement in the neighborhood environment. In response to the priority, the city issued a $10 million bond to finance a plan to eliminate the backlog of dangerous buildings.

As part of the new strategic focus, Kansas City added a dashboard, KCStat (a CitiStat-like program), to publicly track citizen and agency priorities. The online dashboard provides information on high-need issues like crime and healthcare in an easy-to-understand format for any interested resident. The mayor, council, and city manager now hold monthly, open-to-the-public KCStat meetings where they assess progress and discuss new policy directions with an audience of citizens seated in front of them, using up-to-date graphs and maps.

This new data-infused culture is taking root. Citizens and even local TV stations are now accustomed to clicking on the dashboard website and Twitter feed of KCStat metrics to better understand local issues. This open participation in KCStat has helped change the orientation of Kansas City's government from internal to external-oriented, creating a kind of distributed network of citizens, relevant agencies, and local media outlets.

In one telling example, a resident used KCStat data to argue against cutting code-enforcement officers, noting that the city's own numbers showed that each inspector was responsible for more than 300 cases— well above the department's own target of 200. The citizen made the point that fewer inspectors would lead to far less blight removal, one of the city's stated priority areas. Officials reviewed the data, agreed with the analysis, and restored the positions. Another resident tweeted a critique of a chart visualization on KCStat, and the city followed up by bringing her in to teach a data visualization course for city workers.

"This has been an evolution," says Kate Bender, the city's performance manager. "We have created a positive data loop. We have a strategic plan, data around the plan, citizen involvement and the media reporting on our metrics. It is all reinforcing, and it is all focused on what is most important."

THE IMPORTANCE OF RESIDENT INTELLIGENCE

How do citizens get their voice heard in City Hall today? They write a letter or send an email. They call their city council member or leave a comment on his or her Facebook page. Maybe they are one of a handful who attend a hearing or wait to speak at a town hall meeting. Of course even if they make those efforts it's unlikely their input will go far—if one department official gets the message, there isn't much chance they will share it with other agencies.

Cities using a new O/S move from this reporting-and-informing environment to a social platform that produces important insights that advance the quality of life in the city. Collective intelligence requires government to listen in innovative ways, and the more difficult the problem the more comprehensive the managing and monitoring effort needs to be. This shift produces value by incorporating more diverse views earlier and more consistently throughout policy planning efforts. In cities across the country, citizens are already changing and improving government in many ways. These program innovations can be replicated, expanded, and systematized to become an integral part of distributed governance.

Policy Input: Given the usual complexity and implications of policies that guide municipal programs, cities should broadly engage constituents before embarking on any significant policy change. For example, changes in recycling rules, adding new business regulations, or establishing a new program such as school choice vouchers will have profound impact on thousands—perhaps hundreds of thousands—of households. With a robust, thorough way to learn the nuances of how the policies will play out, cities can vastly improve how these policies are written.

When Washington, D.C., wanted to develop an open data policy, the city created drafts.dc.gov using Madison, a government cocreation platform, to learn what people thought about the idea and what it would do. The city encouraged both internal users and the public to comment directly on the proposed policy, receiving 300 comments in four weeks.[3]

Planning: Remaking a city's streetscape or development strategy always provokes comments, but true community intelligence for planning requires an approach—and the tools that support it—to both engage a broader cross section of citizens and to do so in a fashion that guides them to participate in crafting the solution, not just complain about an already achieved result.

One tool for gathering this kind of input is Community PlanIt, an online game platform built by Emerson College's Engagement Lab that helps engage residents in city planning.[4] Several cities have used the game, including Philadelphia for its Philadelphia2035 plan and Boston for its resiliency plan, Climate Smart Boston. When combined with the 3D imaging tools available from GIS, the platform allows residents to model for themselves the effects of a planning decision.

Spending: As discussed in chapter 2, participatory budgeting allows citizens to create ideas and then vote on how certain line items are spent. The same type of process can be used in other ways to give residents a voice in how their tax dollars—or municipal debt—is spent.

For fiscal year 2011, Hampton, Virginia, faced a 5 percent drop in its budget due to a drop in housing-associated revenues. Instead of proposing cuts and waiting for a response, the city asked for public consultation at the front end, aggressively using social media, YouTube videos, online chats, responses to 311, traditional community meetings, and advertisements to learn residents' priorities. These outreach efforts, dubbed I Value, helped educate the public on the choices and gather their "votes" on where to modify budgets. In the end, the proposed cuts generated little opposition and surveys found sizeable increases in citizen satisfaction, the percentage of citizens who thought the city cared about their opinions, and the percentage satisfied with basic city services (90 percent). In a city of 137,000, the simple, well-visualized process involved more than 5,000 participants who identified themselves and an equal number of anonymous participants.

Innovation: In recent years, IT professionals—computer programmers, graphic designers, project managers—have gathered in most large cities for hackathons, using open government data to devise tech-based solutions to civic problems. Their solutions often do not make a significant difference, but the central concept is sound: get interested, creative, knowledgeable people together to brainstorm new ways to solve existing city issues, bringing energy and cutting-edge ideas from the tech world into City Hall.

In New York City, officials have already begun experimenting with how to make the hackathon ethos more effective, using a tech intermediary named Civic Hall to help the app solutions have a deeper impact. Civic Hall surveys residents before the hackathon to better understand street-level needs of a specific area, such as transportation services for seniors. Civic Hall also provides incubation space to ensure that the application is funded, built, and aligned with city agencies and nonprofits. The transition underscores the need for government's role to be carefully crafted, always starting with the problem that needs to be solved, then assisting with locating the right data, and structuring engagement to create a pipeline where ideas can be presented or piloted before a final scaling decision.

Note that the very adoption of the approaches that allow cities to reap these benefits "as part of the policy-making processes constitutes an important organizational innovation for government agencies."[5] In this model, residents not only are providing information to the city, they are getting a promotion from being passive consumers of government products to potentially active members working with their elected leaders. Citizens can move from, in the words of Carolyn Lukensmeyer and L. H. Torres, "users and choosers" of government services to "makers and shapers" of them.[6]

The new O/S will make it easier for persons who share an interest to find out about one another, to work together, and to engage city resources in solving common problems. Erik W. Johnston and Derek L. Hansen, in their work on *Design Lessons for Smart Governance Infrastructures*, describe this process of moving individuals from passive residents to contributors or leaders. Technology can make "user contributions visible to other members, providing low threshold interfaces for easily making micro-contributions . . . giving awards, matching people with mentors or other experts, and providing conditional privileges."[7] For example, a citizen who is complaining about graffiti, trash, and broken sidewalks on a retail street with some empty storefronts can be engaged to take the initiative to connect with his neighbors about the issue and promote an action plan as a group. The result can be the city showing up over a few Saturdays with trash bags, trucks, and shovels to work side-by-side with community members (who have also secured donated paint) to restore the area.

Building a Citizen-Information System

The laundry list of how city departments currently hear from constituents can be considered "push strategies"—the city gets data because a citizen pushes it to government. While this is certainly a legitimate way to add information, it is limited in many ways. Most notably, it is unreliable (residents may or may not weigh in on a topic or at a certain time), unrepresentative (residents who take the time tend to be older, whiter, and better educated), and uneven (hot-button issues may bring in a fair amount of comments, while few people provide input on important but more pedestrian issues).

Every citizen with a smartphone is, in a sense, a potential city inspector whose posted pictures, stamped with time and location, can act as the eyes and ears of the city. Research shows that more than 70 percent of smartphone users share photos and read shared content, so thousands of residents are in a likely position to be nudged to report to authorities wrongdoings or bad experiences at businesses. More cities have the technical capacity to receive smartphone pictures of problems from residents, and increasingly those pictures are integrated in work order systems and available to city workers dispatched to an area, including by apps such as SeeClickFix referenced in chapter 2.

Cities also will need to more systematically pull information from citizens—waiting for residents to decide to tweet or call or visit a website isn't sufficient. To reach out to residents to get their ideas, concerns, and opinions, it is imperative that City Hall both solicit their views in an open, informal basis as well as with organized conversational threads.

Chapter 3 addressed how citizens will receive more customized services in future generations of 311. A corresponding benefit of these enhancements will be platforms that can capture individual and community thoughts and photos about common issues that they want addressed. Citizens will be sharing information concurrently and learning it, as well—posting information on a local condition or issue they care about and being able to see what the city is doing on the topic, as well as what other residents have said. City Hall can also listen and learn by mining unstructured social media for sentiment. For example, tweets that have a geotag can be evaluated to see the presence of certain words that signal an issue—such as a rise in discussion in a specific geographic area about graffiti or broken playground equipment.

Officials can get even more from these sources of information when they initiate campaigns that reach out to communities, asking constituents with SMS signposts to text back a grade for services received, suggest improvements in trash pickup, or grade workforce training services to which they were referred. The city can use other outreach techniques, such as running contests that bring neighbors together around issues of safety or other common concerns. These outreach strategies should be designed to ensure participation by a representative swath of residents, by age, geography, socioeconomic status, race, and ethnicity.

Finally, these community online conversations will be enhanced with quality information from other sources, like environmental sensors that track issues such as noise pollution, air quality, UV levels, or water quality. According to three researchers from Intel and the University of California, Berkeley:

> We claim that these new mobile "sensing instruments" will promote everyday citizens to uncover and visualize unseen elements of their own everyday experiences. As networked devices, they reposition individuals as producers, consumers, and remixers of a vast openly shared public data set. By empowering people to easily measure, report, and compare their own personal environment, a new citizen driven model of civic government can emerge, driven by these new networked-mobile-personal "political artifacts."[8]

The process of listening and learning better will involve an iterative learning progression with a set of steps illustrated in figure 6-1.

1. **Structure the Discussion:** There are many ways to structure online conversations. The city could post a specific challenge that needs to be addressed—from designs for a neighborhood center renovation to the priorities of a capital spending plan—and present relevant data to participants in the discussion in user-friendly formats, such as maps and tables. In some instances, the city will curate the forum, determining whether participants should come from a specific community, for example, or whether to allow

FIGURE 6-1   *Creating Structured Community Input*

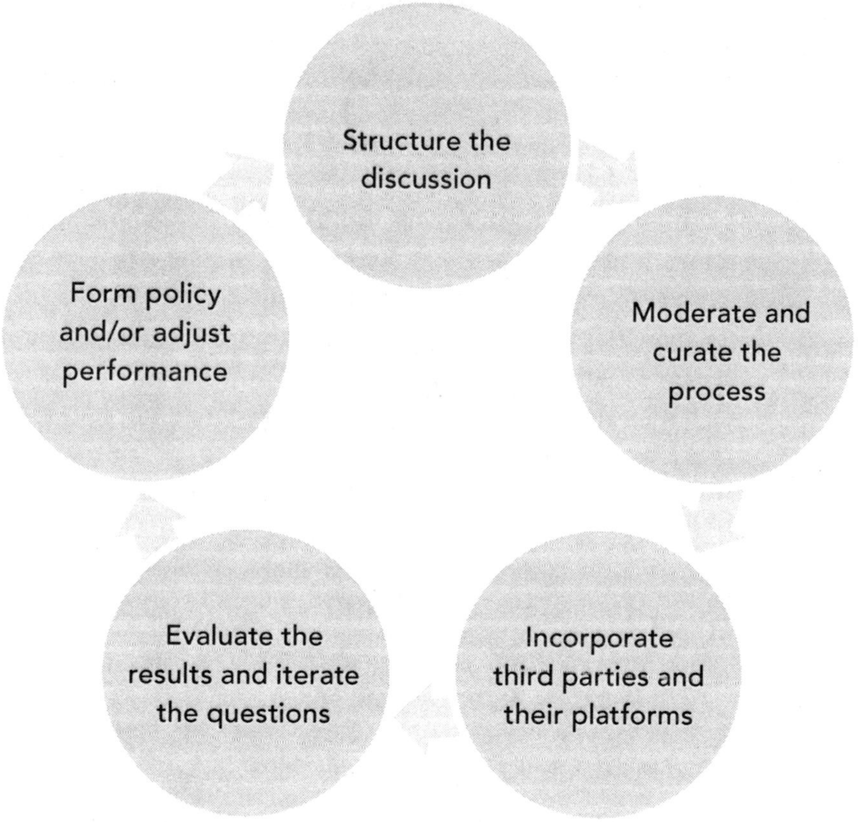

anonymous posting. Systems and rules established by the city should include transparent privacy policies and screen out profanity, anger, ethnic slurs, and the like without crossing the line into censoring the substance. In some situations, the structure could include contests for participants or other ways to enhance or drive the conversation.

2. **Moderate and Curate the Process:** The city should not passively allow a conversation to unfold. It needs to monitor the discussion, organize threads, and when useful, add third-party relevant data. As users generate content, the city can evaluate and index the ideas to insure they are representative. Curation includes making

sure the conversation is inclusive and constructive and deciding when to synthesize and republish the data. Cities should use, depending on the volume of responses, both individuals and machines to evaluate responses and distribute preliminary information to public employees and residents.

3. **Incorporate Third Parties and Their Platforms:** Groups such as community-based organizations, community development corporations, and faith-based coalitions have a long history in many cities and communities of serving as intermediaries between residents and city government, in many cases bringing input from underserved populations. In the new O/S, they can be nodes to bring out residents for collective intelligence programs and/or to curate citizen voices and bring that perspective to the table during discussions. For example, the Smart Chicago Collaborative works with the city and residents to gather their feedback on important issues, as well as to increase the digital literacy of the community groups it serves. As cities are learning how best to build a citizen-information system, libraries are another important resource. In fact, a recent survey of local governments found that 60 percent of cities with populations over 100,000 believed that libraries were a primary venue for engaging residents.[9]

4. **Evaluate Results and Iterate the Questions:** When evaluating results of a conversation, the city can ask additional questions, even changing the original ones based on responses. With machine reading, tens of thousands of responses can be categorized and then visualized in a way that will enhance the continuing discussion. The city can also add other available information to augment the conversation as it evolves. For most projects and policies, officials will need a system to generate, organize, evaluate, and incorporate a continuing loop of information.[10] This system should include a mechanism to provide regular updates to those who participated in the structured conversation (with an easy opt-out option), allowing them to keep track of the progress on the issue they spent time discussing and building trust and ongoing communication with the city.

5. Form Policy and/or Adjust Performance: The municipality uses the responses in shaping the relevant policy. For example, in determining whether an approach to workforce training for an underemployed population is effective, officials would incorporate analysis of the data with ideas from the conversation, particularly areas of widespread agreement or clear importance. An issue concerning, for instance, pedestrian injuries at an intersection could be informed by responses to the city from smartphone outreach, as well as from mining social media.

Moving to these innovative approaches will require not only new systems but also new attitudes from city staff. These structured conversations, if they are to be useful and build new bridges with residents, must be well designed and a true priority for cities.

GOVERNMENT BY PROXY: CONNECTING THE CONTRACTORS

The public good accomplished in a city goes beyond the efforts of public servants. As City Hall organizes its work—from how it identifies what needs to be done to how it organizes the response—it will be working with multiple organizations, often on the same problem at the same time. Some of those individuals will not be part of a formal network; they may be stakeholders or interested nonprofits. Others may be nonprofits and for-profit firms contracted by the city for a broad array of tasks, from infrastructure like treating waste water and laying asphalt to social services like helping domestic violence victims and providing paratransit for seniors.

Because the quality and responsiveness of services delivered by these contractors affects quality of life in the city and the reputation of City Hall, a new O/S must provide the city real-time tools to manage these services. University of Pennsylvania professor John Dilulio, a leading authority on bureaucratic behavior, points out that not only does government feature a poorly trained and short-staffed "acquisition workforce" (those who enter into contracts), but that "civil servants function mainly as grant monitors or contract compliance officers . . . not the proxies' bosses. Rather, each proxy sector—state and local governments, for-profit businesses and nonprofit organizations—has a highly active interest group presence."[11] He prescribes a recipe with more bureaucrats and fewer contractors.

This chapter takes a somewhat different approach, arguing that regardless of the balance between contractors (government by proxy) and bureaucrats, relevant information circulates among all the parties involved in delivering public services and that this web should be managed as a distributed network. When providing services for the city, external contractors and their employees, as well as City Hall, should recognize that they generate valuable data a city can use for its collective intelligence. The difference between a truly distributed system and a more conventional outsourcing contract is not only how information is organized and shared among the official contractors and the city, but also among organizations and individuals who are outside of the contract relationship but who can benefit from that information and also offer the city and contractor important ideas as well.

By incorporating providers into the network of departments and employees discussed in chapter 5, a city can produce a platform that more effectively monitors the results from its contractors, ensuring they remain closely aligned with the goals established by the public agency. Just as important, it adds more information concerning the issue at hand for the benefit of all members of the distributed network.

With robust data and analysis, a nonprofit homeless shelter under contract with the city, for instance, could see patterns that inform its staff when a person under its roof needs domestic violence assistance. Because the shelter would be part of the distributed network, it could also easily see how to get that person connected to the most appropriate services. Sharing information requires guarding privacy—but in many cases simply providing more complete information about someone's circumstances to the frontline workers at the school, agency, or department who are working with an individual or family and authorized to receive the data will enhance results.

The new O/S change in measuring efforts, moving from outputs to outcomes, applies to contractors, as well. Imagine a contract for after-school reading services that is not about the number of children served but about high school graduation rates, or a contract for emergency medical services where the goal is not improved response times but the number of lives saved. For each of these and hundreds of other contracts, government needs a system that can synthesize and analyze data from multiple sources to help officials constantly adjust the contractual outputs in a way that accomplishes the overall goal.

It should be noted that in most situations public officials will struggle with determining the measures, which can be difficult to clearly and confidently establish. In fact, though, the process of this struggle itself will help clarify both the purpose and the terms of the contract. Imagine again in the after-school program, there would be some payment based on children served, since a safe afterschool place is in and of itself an important contribution. Yet the contracting authority, with an overall eye on high school graduation rates, may want to compensate for reading gains as a proxy for that goal.

Contractors may play a role similar to city agencies in many cases, but as separate entities they have an undeniably different relationship with the city. The new O/S needs to provide the rules and technology platform that determines how these government vendors play a part in this network. Communication, clarity, and access to high-quality information sit at the center of coordinated performance.

The O/S must allow for the structuring of information across the network of those who do the city's work for their benefit and that of residents who depend on them for services. Years ago when Indianapolis outsourced the job of towing abandoned cars that were blighting urban neighborhoods, the city benchmarked the contractor's performance to metrics for both how many and how quickly cars were removed. With that incentive in place the city's 911 center started receiving complaints from individuals whose cars had been parked too long but really were not abandoned. In the first contract the city's call center operators had no real-time line of communication with the contractor, so they could only tell irate residents that towing had now been outsourced and they needed to call the contractor. The next iteration of the contract changed the terms of service. City officials gained access to the contractor's information system so police officials could see the location of the vehicle at any time.[12]

The relationships among the city and its contractors need standards that drive outcomes and control the exchange of information in a manner which enables the city to both learn and manage. The O/S should include:

- A glossary of terms used by all relevant parties that will drive data definitions

- Rules on information privacy, security, ownership, and licensing

- Rules on what data should be captured, retained, and shared

- Agreement on dashboards and real-time data visualization

- Contract terms tying data quality and capture to payments

In 2016, the Illinois State Lottery began the process of replacing the private management company contracted to operate its lottery, a multi-billion-dollar game played by hundreds of thousands of residents both online and at retail establishments across the state. Illinois had been one of the first states to enter such a private relationship, but it was fraught with issues related to how the contract was structured. As the new governor's lawyers began the process of writing specs for the RFP, they discovered that critical pieces of information belonged exclusively to the contractor, including the demographics of individuals playing specific games and how and when players interacted with the lottery.

With access, the state could have data that allowed it to see if the lottery was inappropriately directing its marketing at lower-income communities or problem gamblers, or it could determine where high numbers of transactions occur at kiosks, suggesting that an omni-channel approach that also offers other state services at that location would be effective. In the RFP issued to select a new private manager, the state clearly specified that all information produced from the contract belonged to it, with a use license to the vendor, giving state contract managers real-time information to better manage contract deliverables, audit financials, and evaluate performance.

The Harvard Kennedy School Government Performance Lab supports outcome-driven procurements. Its definition of active contract management says:

The processes of sharing and reviewing data on a regular basis and making collaborative decisions and changes based on those data. A foundation of reliable, relevant, and trustworthy data can ensure that key stakeholders operate with a common understanding of performance and can illuminate trends [that drive] program adjustments and policy decisions. [Government] will use performance data to collaborate with providers to monitor progress, detect problems, and resolve issues in real time.[13]

The work of a city involves a broad array of individuals. An operating system that integrates this information, turns it into useable knowledge, and turns that knowledge into better, more responsive services will be adding to that reservoir of trust that helps enhance the quality of community life.

GREATER CAPACITY WITH INSTITUTIONAL PARTNERS

By any measure, cities need help making the transition to the new O/S that affords discretion to frontline workers while simultaneously knitting together third parties to take on tough systemic issues. Traditional institutions and actors need to—and in many cases, have begun to— play a much larger and key role as city partners.

Universities and Other Key Local Institutions

For most cities, "anchor institutions"—universities, medical centers, and hospitals—are critical partners for building a distributed governance. Almost every city is home to several such institutions, and they are increasingly the largest job generators locally, part of fast-growing sectors like engineering, bioscience, and healthcare.[14] Beyond being a critical economic engine, many anchor institutions have become far more involved in citywide systems and strategies, sitting down with City Hall leaders and collaborating around new growth efforts for the region. Traditionally, anchor institution involvement with the world outside its campus was strictly limited to the surrounding city blocks, a form of "enlightened self-interest" that, in some cases, could also be negatively seen as gentrifying a neighborhood and adding to the polarized town/ gown dynamic.

Across the country, though, many more universities and hospitals are exploring how they can complement and support mayors and city managers on ambitious new municipal turnaround plans. In Wilkes-Barre, Pennsylvania, the presidents of King's College and Wilkes University worked hand-in-glove with the mayor to vastly improve a moribund downtown by coordinating real estate projects and financing of related development efforts. In Providence, Rhode Island, Brown University has begun working with the mayor on early childhood literacy, and in Waco, Texas, Baylor University and local hospitals have collaborated with the mayor and city manager to develop strategies to retain college graduates and boost public school attainment. These ambitious efforts signal a much-improved environment for cities to work with anchors as partners in a wider distributed network of local policy and service delivery.[15]

David Eichenthal, managing director at the consulting firm PFM Group, has worked with dozens of cities and notes that the relationship between City Hall and anchor institutions has gotten much better in recent years:

> Imagine if you said to a local mayor that it was a "bad thing" to be talking to your local business community. They would look at you like you're insane, as almost all of them have strong ties with local businesses. But by the same token, few of them have that kind of relationship with their local university or hospital. That has begun to shift, as cities are realizing that they are an obvious partner, especially as governing has become more complicated.

Even more relevant for administering a new O/S, a few anchor institutions have begun managing sophisticated evaluation and data analytic programs with and for city government. The Urban Labs program at the University of Chicago has taken on five core areas (education, crime, poverty, health, and energy/environment) and created centers that are explicitly tied to and serve City Hall for each topic. Run by leading experts in each field, the UChicago Urban Labs use administrative data and newly designed experiments to give local leaders rigorous studies of which programs are most effective and how they should be improved. "This is a mutually beneficial framework. By leveraging what we do well to support communities and neighbors, we are all better off," says Derek Douglas, vice president for civic engagement and external affairs at the University of Chicago.

In 2011 New York City mayor Michael Bloomberg launched an Applied Sciences Competition to spur more engineering programming in the city. New York University was one of the winners and created the Center for Urban Science and Progress (CUSP), the first academic program in the country to be established as part of city/university MOU (memorandum of understanding). CUSP is both an academic and practice-based program that serves important city data needs. Instructors have been recruited worldwide for their ability to analyze big datasets and provide agencies with insights and direction.

One promising initiative is the Quantified Community, a partnership between New York University and the de Blasio administration targeting data strategies in selected neighborhoods, including Red Hook and Brownsville. Perhaps the most ambitious effort is being conducted in partnership with private developers building out the twenty-eight-acre Hudson Yards Project, one of the largest new business districts in the world, with sixteen new skyscrapers and a planned 750,000 square feet of retail space. Beginning in 2016, the Urban Intelligence Lab at CUSP began collecting all sensor and administrative-based data on pedestrian traffic, air quality, energy production and consumption, and even the health and activity levels of workers and residents. By working with the city and private partners, CUSP will add to the collective intelligence of the city, with an ability to better determine utility and green space use and how best to organize core public safety and health services based on aggregate and real-time data.

Philanthropy's Expanding Role

Foundations have long supported urban initiatives, from affordable housing to community health care to public education. Over the last twenty years or so, however, many national foundations have begun working more actively in cities, partnering both with municipal leaders and community organizations around shared priorities. For example, the Annie E. Casey Foundation funded a groundbreaking effort to deliver technology solutions to child welfare workers through its Casebook program and supports a range of projects that leverage data to improve urban areas, such as Kids Count, which maintains the best state-by-state data available about children's well-being. Bloomberg Philanthropies has a portfolio of programs that support innovation teams, data-driven decision making, behavioral insights, leadership development, and more—and is pushing cities to braid these efforts together. And the Laura and John Arnold Foundation has made a major investment in using data to address inequities and inefficiencies in criminal justice and jails.

In some cities, local foundations have begun to play a far more strategic role, as well, supporting efforts where local government is weak. In northeast Ohio, for instance, the Cleveland Foundation funded economic studies to determine how Case Western University, the Cleveland Clinic, and University Hospitals could best support local business development and job training.

Leading national foundations are still exploring how deep their role with cities can go. In 2010 Rip Rapson, the CEO of The Kresge Foundation, took well-respected urban planner Toni Griffin to dinner. Griffin, a consultant and professor in the Graduate School of Design at Harvard, had served as vice president and director of design for the effort to transform the once neglected Anacostia area of southeast Washington, D.C. Rapson had a proposition for her: come to Detroit and lead a community-driven process to provide options for the future of Detroit—essentially draft a plan for reimagining how and where to strategically invest Detroit's limited public resources to best catalyze investment and strengthen the city.

This comprehensive and action-oriented blueprint was funded by Kresge and other national philanthropies, including the Ford, Kellogg, and Knight Foundations. Its twenty-four-month planning process included more than fifty community organizers using numerous strategies to connect with residents 163,000 times to create a true citizen vision.

Resident ideas formed the basis of the framework, which was then written by a team of technical experts in areas ranging from economic development to landscape architecture, who supported the residents' ideas with evidence-based strategies and proven programs from other locales. This thorough thinking was critical for a plan that addressed core areas such as infrastructure and economic development while also taking on politically charged issues like perpetual population and job loss, repurposing land in ways outside of traditional community development, and creating a system of city services that aligns with future land use projections. Today, private, public, and philanthropic sectors ground investments through the tenets of the Detroit Future City framework. Rapson reflects, "As our nation's front-line problem-solvers, municipal governments are substituting innovation, flexibility, and collaboration for a stale command-and-control mentality that effectively walled out the private, nonprofit, civic, and philanthropic sectors. We've seen in Detroit how transformative that mind-shift can be in confronting, and chipping away at, a community's most stubbornly persistent challenges."

The foundations mentioned here and others increasingly play a catalytic role in America's cities, providing impact investments from focused philanthropy initiatives that build local governance capacity. Foundations don't have the same profit motives as the private sector—allowing them to fill critical financing gaps—and can work on a longer time horizon than elected officials. This makes them a natural financing partner for "venture capital" for city government innovation and also a natural candidate to be a leader on important longer-term projects and initiatives that city government does not have the bandwidth or time horizon to easily deliver. In this respect, foundations are both part of the distributed system and part of the infrastructure that supports it, playing a unique role alongside the private and nonprofit sectors in helping government.

Chantel Rush, a program officer at Kresge who helps lead the foundation's urban agenda, says:

This model of distributed leadership has many benefits. It allows us to tackle multiple civic issues at once, it leverages the full breadth of our civic institutions, putting them each to work, and it allows us to benefit from each institution's unique strengths and capabilities—for example, philanthropy's ability to take on risk and the private sector's skills and resources.[16]

These partnerships work only if cities enter them with their own priorities clearly spelled out. Do they need assistance with data mining, economic development planning, or reorganization assistance for a new government O/S? It is, then, incumbent on the city to see how their priorities align with external partners. Foundations do not want to be treated like an ATM and universities need outlets for research. City priorities and those of external partners can align easily enough, but the time must be put into clarifying and consistently managing the relationship.

Chapter 6   **THE BOTTOM LINE**

Key Points

- A new distributed operating system supports strong and highly coordinated relationships outside of City Hall. More outreach to and alignment with communities, residents, and partners like universities and local foundations are needed.

- Distributed governance allows government to coordinate services that reach more individuals more responsively and with more legitimacy in the way they are delivered.

- By turning outward, cities can vastly expand their knowledge base from one that is limited to a small set of agency metrics to one that is widely informed by stakeholders beyond the walls of City Hall.

- Some cities have already begun to listen more closely to residents in areas like planning and spending—showing the benefit of social engagement and input—but these concepts must be woven much more deeply into government operations.

Pitfalls

- Do not confuse traditional public/private partnerships (governing by network) with distributed governance. The former is about outside entities contracted to deliver a specific service; the latter is about establishing roles and rules for communications, conduct, quality, equity, and privacy among actors.

- Move away from conditions where contracted services from third parties do not produce needed information. The relationships among the city and its contractors need standards that will enable the city to both manage and learn from services delivered.

Recommendations

- Adding citizen input to a city's collective intelligence can benefit from technology such as smartphones and new 311 centers to improve push and pull strategies, where citizens contact government with ideas and opinions.

- Structured discussions, where the city works to solicit citizen opinion on critical issues, must a) be well managed, b) include active listening and moderation of discussions, c) include trusted intermediaries such as libraries and civic tech and neighborhood organizations, d) evaluate results and change course based on what the data says, and, finally, e) change policy or adjust performance.

Examples

- By orienting government reform and data gathering around citizen interests, Kansas City has created a new civic culture of residents keeping track of and, in turn, helping shape city reform that is assessed through rigorous data gathering.

- Universities and foundations are assuming a significant municipal role in places like Detroit, Michigan (foundation-funded research of a citywide turnaround plan); Wilkes-Barre (local universities partnering around major downtown redevelopment); and New York City (university-led data science programming makes local development "smarter" and more efficient).

NOTES

1. Stephen Goldsmith and William Eggers, *Governing by Network* (Brookings Institution Press, 2004).

2. Jeremy Millard, "Open Governance Systems: Doing More With More," *Government Information Quarterly* (September 2015), p. 9.

3. Stephen Larrick and Alyssa Doom interview with Matt Bailey, "How to Invite Feedback on an Open Data Policy," *Sunlight Foundation*, March 10, 2017 (https://sunlightfoundation.com/2017/03/10/how-to-invite-feedback-on-an -open-data-policy).

4. See Engagement Lab, "Community PlanIt" (https://elab.emerson.edu /projects/civic-media/community-planit).

5. Enrico Ferro and others, "Policy Making 2.0: From Theory to Practice," *Government Information Quarterly* 30 (2013), p. 359.

6. Carolyn J. Lukensmeyer and L. H. Torres, "Citizensourcing: Citizen Participation in a Networked Nation," in *Civic Engagement in a Network Society*, edited by Kaifang Yang and Erik Bergrud (Charlotte, N.C.: Information Age Publishing, 2008), pp. 207–33.

7. Erik W. Johnston and Derek L. Hansen, "Design Lessons for Smart Governance Infrastructures," in *Transforming American Governance: Rebooting the Public Square*, edited by Alan Balutis and others (New York: Routledge, 2011), pp. 3–40.

8. Erik Paulos, R. J. Honicky, and Ben Hooker, "Citizen Science: Enabling Participatory Urbanism," *Urban informatics: Community Integration and Implementation*, edited by Marcus Foth (London: Information Science Reference, 2008), p. 416.

9. John B. Horrigan, "The Role of Libraries in Advancing Community Goals," Aspen Institute, 2017 (https://assets.aspeninstitute.org/content/uploads /2017/01/AspenICMAReport-1-13-17.pdf).

10. Erika Deckers and Taulbee Jackson, *The Owned Media Doctrine: Marketing Operations Theory, Strategy* (Bloomington, Ind.: Archway Publishing, 2013).

11. John J. Dilulio, *Bring Back the Bureaucrats* (West Conshohocken, Pa.: Templeton Press, 2014), p. 26.

12. Goldsmith and Eggers, *Governing by Network*, p. 101.

13. Christine Grover-Roybal and Hanna Azemati, "Shaking up the Routine: How Seattle Is Implementing Results-Driven Contracting Practices to Improve Outcomes for People Experiencing Homelessness," *Harvard Kennedy School Government Performance Lab* (September 2016), p. 8.

14. Beth Dever and others, "Anchors Lift All Boats: Eds & Meds Engaging with Communities," *Lincoln Institute of Land Policy*, February 2015 (www.lincolninst.edu/publications/articles/anchors-lift-all-boats).

15. Neil Kleiman and others, "Striking a (Local) Grand Bargain," *National Resource Network* (September 2015).

16. Chantel Rush, "Making the New Urban Agenda a Reality: Lessons on Implementation from Detroit" (speech, UN Habitat III: Next City World Stage, Quito, Ecuador, October 17, 2016).

SEVEN

A New City from a New O/S

This book presents a path for better governance, one that recognizes the vast changes in society and communications that demand equally vast changes in how we govern. The Progressive reform movement designed command-and-control systems to prevent corruption. Tight control of information, work organized around routines and rules, and a professional class of bureaucrats significantly improved things over the ward heelers of Boss Tweed. Closed government now must give way to open governance, where the public can clearly see its information, once hoarded in a file cabinet in City Hall, and where the new definition of *professional* is less an elite and more a synthesizer of wisdom generated from multiple sources, including other agencies, residents, nonprofits, and for-profit contractors.

A new operating system for government leverages modern technologies by designing responses around the citizen and the employee that allows government to act in time. The new system focuses on results by automating routine work and providing employees more discretion and more decision support tools. It involves community collaboration in much more far-reaching ways. We find pieces of these building blocks in cities all over the country—in some cases fairly large pieces—but no City Hall has yet incorporated everything or brought them into alignment to operate as a citywide O/S.

Chapter by chapter, this book has examined the components and concepts that, once assembled, work in concert to allow governance to be more open, employees to have more discretion, and citizens to trust in and partner with their city. Because the new O/S is so new, it made sense to deeply explore the code behind the operating system. What will it be like to see it in full operation? To get a vision of how your city could be running in a few years, consider a speculative description of a day in the life of a fictional mayor.

Although I became mayor after a stint on the city council, by profession I am a lawyer. That does not automatically disqualify me from managing the city as a business, but it doesn't necessarily qualify me for the job as an executive, either. That's fine; I don't really want to run the city like a business. I do, though, constantly consider whether our city is investing its resources in the right way, and I want to use business approaches to run the city as a city. I think that's important to reach our goal: inclusively, fairly, and effectively turning the messiness of democracy, often stirred up by competing stakeholders, into policies that help people.

At first I thought of our residents as customers. While some of them are sort of like customers, others who owe the city money or commit a crime have an additional relationship, as well. Struggling residents who receive government services to improve their lives are customers in a much more limited way, in the sense that they don't have much choice concerning how or from whom they get help. But if the concept of citizens as customers isn't quite right, it does get to the idea that everyone deserves effective services, designed around them

I take some real pride in the fact that I incorporated the best available technology when modernizing our systems. I want to be known as having the best local government in the country. This Tuesday morning, as I'm being driven to work early, I worry because we're having the fifth straight day of rain, which sometimes means that streets will flood and sewers overflow. On my phone I look at a map of the hardest-hit areas. It used to be that my phone could access broad performance data from the fancy dashboards the IT department provided; in some cases it had real-time data, but most of the information was from the last quarter. It always felt like, except for an occasional alert, it took too long to dig out the facts I needed.

Now, with a couple of clicks, the map can show me if we have serious problems this morning and where, fed from alerts generated by sensors in the sewer. A while back, if I started a day early enough, I would alert city crews and commissioners to problems, but now I don't bother; they've got their own versions of these maps and they're always ahead of me. Mary, who manages the new 311 call center, has set it up so that a bot automatically reads the sensor data and alerts a registry of citizens who have asked for notices of problems in their neighborhood or along their routes to work or school. Parents can also sign up for real-time tracking information about their children's school bus, so they will receive customized alerts from their school, as well.

Mary is one of the best public servants I've worked with. I've spent some time in her citizen contact center, so I can picture what it's like on a busy day like today. The call center now offloads routine calls to a bot, which allows the contact center operators time for them to focus on responding to the more complicated questions posed by calls, tweets, and app requests. Today that means the operators have the capacity to really work with residents who report problems like water in their basements. I'm glad citizens who have a knotty problem get through more quickly to a representative, and one who has access to a lot more good information about what to do. Those are folks who're going to have a good story, not a complaint, to tell at work about what happened when they called the city.

These are the kind of days that really show off what we get from mining real-time public social media traffic like tweets, WhatsApp, and Facebook postings. Mary worked with our data analyst and designers to incorporate this social media information into the highly visual open data maps the agents use in responding to questions. Many worried homeowners today will be using our open data portal on their own mobile devices to view the same maps now being displayed on the screens in the contact center. (We stole this idea from New York City.) All the

data is open; it's just that each of us sees what is available specially configured for us and our purposes—the resident for their neighborhood, the
call center operator for the area of the city and the departments with
which she is working, and the most hard-hit areas for me.

My police officer driver makes a turn that surprises me; he explains
the 911 center received an alert generated from a Waze feed about a tree
that fell and is blocking a street on what would typically have been our
route. Although all Wazers can now take advantage of this two-way feed,
our emergency dispatchers seem to use it particularly well for rerout-
ing ambulances—and for me today, evidently. (This one is an idea we
stole from Los Angeles and Boston.) I'm glad we didn't get stuck there;
my time always matters to me—just like everyone, I suppose. But the
first item on my schedule today is a community breakfast meeting for
public input on a new development, and I really don't want to be late.
These kinds of meetings have such a different feel than they used to. I
look forward to them now!

When I get to the Windale Community Center, about a hundred
people are ready to discuss what I know is a controversial request for a
zoning variance for a nearby parcel of land that would allow a larger
building to be constructed. The variance would produce tax revenue
and needed housing, but park advocates are saying it would also put the
playground in unpleasant shadows much of the day. The Parks and Economic Development directors join me at the meeting, and they also share
differences about the project. In this instance, though, we anticipate a
productive meeting that will take us to some sort of resolution.

In the past, meetings like this created more heat than light. Residents would imagine the worst and express those objections loudly
and, in a lot of cases, rudely. I guess when you think you have one chance
to be heard you try to be as memorable as possible. In preparation for
this meeting, for the last month everyone in the room has been able to
watch the interactive posting of comments on the project, as neighbors
have responded to each other and to us. We now provide community groups
with easy-to-use software so they can visualize real-life consequences—
in this instance by adjusting the height of the building by time of day
and season, so they can see what parts of the park would, in fact, be in

the shadows. (We stole this idea from Philadelphia.) It's surprisingly easy to use—they showed me how to add in tree foliage by time of year, as well.

The Windale Center looks like many such places in transitional neighborhoods: older, with paint peeling here or there, but clean. Clearly it's an organization that takes pride in its community. Today it really feels like the future and the past have merged, as the wood-paneled room is hung with large screens that project the plans and organized discussion threads about specific issues that need to be resolved. Once we get going not everyone in the conversation presents themselves in a scientific way, but I think having specifics in front of us all makes a real difference.

When we leave an hour later, I sense the discussion has ended with a convergence of views around a settlement that involves slightly moving the building, reducing its size some, and shifting a couple of the angles. After last year's community meetings, where about two dozen of the 300 people present took turns yelling at me, I feel like we found a better way to engage much more broadly with our residents, even when they disagree with each other and me. And the fact that everything was open—maps, planner comments, neighborhood views, and even visualizations of what might occur—defused a sense of suspicion and cynicism that the whole event was just for show.

As the center director escorts me out of the building, he's excited to point out some construction work in a small playground across the street. We operate a matching grant program with a third-party crowd-funding tool that posts parks and public spaces projects and creates a community fundraising campaign. In this case, the businesses and neighbors in Windale and interested foundations came up with $100,000, which triggered the city's contribution, and now the playground revitalization work has started. (This idea was borrowed from Michigan.)

I have a staff meeting this afternoon, and I usually stop first at the city's performance management center, so that will be our next destination. I can see the city analysis on my phone's customized dashboard and, with a bit of work, can sort the metrics by district and department. I usually look at customer satisfaction scores and response time by peer groups to get an idea of which street department district supervisor is doing the best or worst job. But since we altered the performance center's mission and made it a data analytics center, I can now be even better prepared for the staff meeting.

We rebuilt the room for this team. Our City Hall office building is a bit dingy (not the mayor's office, of course) and doesn't look modern at all. I wanted the surroundings for the geeks to be different—both for recruitment and to make a statement to the rest of government. Symbols are important and this one particularly so. Monitors on the walls and cubicles (no offices) fill the room, each displaying a map or visualization of a result or score. (We took this idea from Indiana.) Tammy, the chief data officer, and her team no longer just track metrics, though; now they also identify outliers, predict problems, and get us a handle on issues that cannot be solved with just the focus of one agency.

Those metrics on the screens are new, as well, the result of redoing last year what we count as accomplishments. Way too many of our measurements before were just checking off activities from an agency's annual list: homeless beds provided, emergency room visits processed. That didn't really tell us much about whether things were really improving for people. For each agency, we identified its goals in terms of public value; how that value amplified the vision I had announced of a healthy, competitive, and equitable city; and how the agency's work (inputs) drove that value. Now metrics are things like the rate of high school graduates who attend college, how many of our citizens are homeless, the state of health of our residents—and those metrics, in turn, have more detailed objectives that, if accomplished, will drive those results.

In this stop before my staff meeting, though, I'm particularly interested in something I can't see on my dashboard: the questions they'll have about this rainfall. Some of the Public Works and Transportation supervisors should have been working with the data geeks to dig deeper into what would make a difference for our flooding project. I am looking for an example of a creative employee who has been asking questions about his own district. Do historic flooding patterns accurately predict where there have been problems the last few days? What about some strategies that we tried—street-cleaning modifications, new types of grates, extra trees and roadway plantings? Does the data show that any of that helped? Did anyone think to ask whether the sensors we spent so much on gave us a heads-up, so we could divert water before it flooded? I want to identify a worker who took the data and solved a problem, to highlight his or her work.

It's part of a whole new mindset to reward results. Performance does not merely mean how quickly we respond to a flooded street but whether we prevent it in the first place. To free our employees to focus on results, we took all those ridiculous forms and the mindless work we used to have them do and reassigned most of it to machines to read and fill out. We retrained many our employees and constantly recognize and reward them for their problem-solving—for the outcomes they produce.

I worry, though, whether our top-down push to change government has been successful in unleashing the bottom-up creativity we had envisioned. I had tasked Tammy with advancing and supporting data literacy for the ranks of our employees. (We took this idea from San Francisco.) Every month my deputy mayor holds a meeting with the data analytics center director and all the agency chief operating officers to discuss and highlight how they use data to solve problems. But that's not sufficient. We really need broader and deeper use of data throughout the city workforce. Every government employee should be asking "what if" questions: what if I changed this approach; what if I changed this route; what if I teamed up with this other agency.

I'm also preparing for a briefing on another initiative—an update on an important transportation issue. Just a few years ago we had separate departments or agencies for transportation, transit, taxi and shared rides, and biking and walking. This seemed to me to represent exactly how government should not work—several agencies touching the elephant in various places with no concept of what the elephant looked like. But reorganizing government agencies never motivated me much—it involves legislative, space, and people issues that introduce too much chaos. Now, because of various reforms, including our intelligence hub, we have totally open data, and we geotag almost everything, so no matter where you are in government or what you are working on, you can see the plans and activities of others relating to the same location. It lets us create virtual teams without the organizational effort.

So for today's staff meeting the question to be addressed is how underemployed individuals can get from the Belmont neighborhood to the job clusters advertising for labor. (We took this idea from NYC and LA) We all can see the maps that show the problem and the unfortunately too vivid demonstration of our challenges. To get a handle on the system that needs to respond to transportation problems like this, I recruited Tom to coordinate mobility—not buses, taxis, cars, or bikes, but mobility. The data team will present its findings on how we can use shared rides to augment transit in Belmont, and Tom will present his recommendation to the team.

On so many of these issues, just four years ago we not only lacked coordination but actionable intelligence. We made three big changes that powered many of the insights. We started considering mobility as a system rather than its individual parts. We put together data from all the modes, and we involved users of the system. In our improved process, we have surveyed neighbors, both in community meetings and through an SMS app where we posted signs—at bus stops, grocery stores, and barbershops, for instance—asking questions about transit needs and wants. We then merged that information, analyzed it and visualized it, and presented suggestions that I am now watching at the meeting.

By the way, I was proud of the way Alice, our HR director, filled the mobility job. From the time we decided to create the position until Alice offered it to Tom was thirty days. A day to write the description, a week to post it on Idealist, and then interviews. The era of civil service tests, archaic classification procedures, and the like should be fully discarded to the dustbin. Alice has collapsed job classifications even for the field jobs. She uses her own and third-party data to determine which backgrounds most frequently lead to productive long-term employees. She tailors training to employees based on metrics. Because our employees have so much more authority to problem-solve, they're much more satisfied with their jobs and have higher morale. It also means we really must up our game for high-quality training—both on approaches to the job and the technologies available. (We took this idea from Denver.)

The same kind of mentality of working across agencies is also part of my big meeting tomorrow with criminal justice officials to talk about the fact that our jail is overcrowded. It's not just that the facility might be getting unsafe; there is no reason for many of those individuals to be there in the first place. The district attorney, sheriff, and judges all have differing views of what to do about it. I asked our data team to help me prepare by gathering all available information to show the results from each of the relevant actions taken by some official in the system—who is arrested or summonsed in lieu of arrests, whom do they release on bail, how long do we hold individuals by race and wealth—and for each of these decisions, what effect does it have on future criminality. The city and criminal justice officials today manage a range of programs, like GED prep, job training, and drug interventions, but I really need to know which of those programs and in which combinations make a difference for which populations. Instead of arguing with the other officials about what might happen if we change a policy, the data team can model it for me.

We have several more of these cross-agency working groups, focused on issues ranging from affordable housing and homelessness to income inequality, and each is supported by a team of data-savvy geeks coordinated out of the analytics center but chaired by my deputy mayor or me with an assigned top-level program manager. Now that we're looking at these issues from many perspectives at once, these working groups can share what they've learned from talking with their constituents, too. For income inequality, for instance, ideas from focus groups with students at the local community college are mixed with surveys of job seekers who are having a particularly hard time finding employment in combination with what our economic development department knows from surveys of local small businesses and employers in our region's growing economic clusters.

As you can imagine, many of these complex issues require deep expertise to support the policy analysis. These working groups have produced some interesting partnerships with professors and departments at the university whose research and analytical backgrounds greatly aid our policy discussions. (We took this idea from Chicago.) In addition, several of the university departments have placed interns in various city offices, which provides us with more capacity—and my hope is that some of those students see city government as an exciting career option once they graduate.

You should see our data-savvy police department. I spent a night with a few of my officers last month, and fortunately the days of police driving around aimlessly hoping to stumble onto something are over. I rode with some officers and walked around with others, and none had much free time. To explore activity in their precincts, they were constantly using the tablets we had installed in the cars or using their smartphones when walking a beat. Sophisticated algorithms work with various record systems and sensors to send them customized notices.

While I was there, the tablet told the officers that a stolen vehicle might be headed in their direction—license plate readers triggered that alert. Later that night, the officers were poised to enter a house in response to a report about a loud argument. After some rapid tapping on their phones, they told me the address was the last known location of a suspect who had beat up his girlfriend three previous times and who also was involved in a very nasty confrontation with an officer two weeks ago a couple blocks away. It turned out he wasn't home, but it was good to know the cops had a lot of information about what they might encounter. A couple of times that night it was gratifying to see residents in high-crime areas confidentially text one of the officers with some news about the block. I know not many people living in these areas feel comfortable calling a faceless department, so having a relationship with a specific officer is a good way to build trust with law enforcement and for the police to know more about the blocks they patrol. (We took this approach from NYC.)

I asked the chief after that visit if he had set me up with particularly good officers. He did confess that, well of course they were among the better cops, but he added quickly that they weren't unique and he said that's, in part, because hiring and training processes had really improved. He uses data to identify police candidates with the right characteristics, and that has cut the time for recruiting and testing and hiring in half. He also said the department has a much easier time determining if an officer has problematic attitudes. Rather than waiting to determine the significance of an isolated complaint, department officials use data derived from many sources, including case notes and broadcasts and the number of stress-related events in which officers have been involved. Some police need training, others need time off, others need to see a counselor, but the chief believes we are, overall, changing the composition and skill level of the officers.

Anyway, finished with the staff meeting. I am off to one of my most important events today—a ribbon-cutting, complete with, I hope, plenty of smiling people. This event celebrates a new midsize office building, which we safely permitted in record time. We have a campaign to convince city employees that time equals money. Lost time costs merchants and those who will invest in our city, and it costs us tax dollars.

Of course none of this matters to the beleaguered public employee if she has so much work to do that the concept of timely responses is a futile goal. But things are changing rapidly. Every project and every developer and contractor who requests a permit gets a score based on the complexity of the project and the record of the developer in terms of any previous issues or citations of any sort—safety, tax payments, OSHA issues, community benefit arrangements fulfilled, and so on. The simple project gets in and out of the permit office in less than an hour (borrowed from Atlanta). Complicated projects get submitted to coordinated cross-agency teams that work together on a virtual file.

The most rewarding moment for me at the ribbon-cutting wasn't the thanks from the well-known developer—I kind of expected that. It was from the immigrant owner of the coffee shop that's part of the building's first floor retail. He told me that it's his third storefront café, and that means that right now his capital is spread a bit thin in such a low-margin business. For this location he said he couldn't have been happier about what it took to get a restaurant license: one stop, one form. The other times, he needed ten different licenses from the fire, buildings, and health departments and the like, spending weeks running around and waiting to have any paying customers. He added with a big smile that it appeared we had a designed a system with him, the user, in mind (which we did; we ran a number of focus groups and business surveys with small business owners as part of our policy reform process). He said he wanted me to know that he didn't object to our standards, but he had objected to the process he experienced for the first two stores that delayed his opening by nine months, which cost him a lot of money.

He invited me in for a muffin proudly saying he has never received a health citation and that now the health inspectors seemed to have a totally different attitude in engaging him. When I asked him what he meant he said the better he performs the less frequently they appear and that when they do stop by, they come with a tablet that contains everything about him and his stores—whether he has violations or complaints registered, what people say about him on Yelp. That makes everything go much easier. (We took this idea from Chicago.)

We have a long way to go, but I feel like we are making progress. Our community is connected and engaged. We take care not to just put up open data but to organize and visualize it by themes so more people can make use of it. We have not replaced several of our supervisors who retired because our employees make more of their own decisions each day. The current managers have better digital tools to watch the accomplishments of their employees, seeing not only who is producing more but insuring that they speak with and treat people with respect and fairly no matter what community they're serving.

This city still has significant problems dealing with poverty, inequality, and the need to better turn ethnic differences from challenges to assets, but I can safely say that we now operate in a way that leads to more responsiveness, more satisfied employees, and a community that trusts its government. This is the emergence of the trust and political capital that will allow our city to not only take on large, important social and economic issues but to create solutions that are going to keep making the city a place anyone would want to live and work and play. We are pleased to be known as the city of the near future.

APPENDIX

Implementation Guide

Strategies to Address the Ten Most
Important Challenges to a New O/S

Cities that move to a new operating system will encounter difficulties and face resistance, as would be expected for such a wide-ranging, systemic change. Yet executive leadership and dedicated managers can overcome these challenges. This road map identifies the major barriers likely to come into play—some large, some more minor, and all dependent to some degree on the specific circumstances in place for each local government—and presents policies and approaches local leaders can use to establish a new O/S, despite these factors.

The Leadership Challenge

The new O/S demands strong and adaptive leadership to institute an entirely new approach for government workers. Change will not occur organically, as agencies will likely push back against a new system that, in many ways, runs counter to standard operating procedures.

Recommended Solutions

- Make a leadership mix of vision, operations, and engagement a priority, balancing the capacity to articulate a rousing vision, oversee operational detail, and recruit top-level teams that blend complementary skills.

- Advance a robust engagement strategy by ensuring leadership is attuned in a tangible way to ideas that flow from the bottom up and from the outside in.

- Provide all government staff a dashboard customized to their position that visualizes goals, performance metrics, and peer results.

- Lead sessions with senior managers on aspects of the new O/S to expand the imagination of city officials in how they address problems and use helpful implementation frameworks like Equipt to Innovate as a resource.

- Use social media and a dedicated section of the city's website to extol the success of mid-level and frontline workers.

The Financial Challenge

A city may find it difficult to dedicate initial funding for a new O/S. Few cities have development funds for new initiatives, and agencies will protect their existing program budgets. Although upfront costs for change management may require higher expenses in the short term, once established, a new O/S will produce more effective spending and savings from smarter operations from new data and analytics that will offset other expenses.

Recommended Solutions

- Defuse potential controversy with a public statement about the new O/S that makes it clear that the system is a new social "compact" that will increase customer satisfaction and government ef-

ficiency while protecting current government jobs and improving services.

- Evaluate programs, internal or run by contractors, with the stat
and data analytics teams to determine which funds are effective and which can be redeployed to build up O/S capacity and
advance core outcomes. Make this information available to the
public.

- Establish gain-sharing programs that allow employees who generate ideas that save the city money a share of the measured savings once their ideas are implemented.

- Use creative tools to save money and improve fidelity to outcomes,
such as the Pay for Success performance-based contracting model.

The Collaboration Challenge

Local government is based on hierarchical organization and systems of
control, and government employees (by training and experience) are
used to operating nearly exclusively within their departments. The new
O/S requires public servants to work and coordinate with federal and
state governments above, relevant agencies and citizens across, and their
frontline workers below. Cities must change culture and supporting IT
to convert a stovepipe organizational structure to one that collectively
tackles big problems. Local government must require agencies to listen
and act differently than they have for generations.

Recommended Solutions

- Create digital scaffolding that contains platforms for inter-
department and cross-government collaboration, similar to the
GeoHub in Los Angeles.

- Require that all documents and photos contain tags by geography
(GIS) and/or subject matter (for example, sustainability), allowing
most information to be easily located and connected.

- Task every agency to develop specific listening and collaboration plans with other agencies that combine regular meetings, social media, and collaborative outreach to communities.

- Require that prior to implementing any new rule agencies post the problem on a site that makes it easy for interactive social commentary from interested stakeholders.

The Challenge to Define Performance

To establish wide-ranging distributed governance, a city must peg performance to outcomes, providing clarity to hold the disparate parts of a distributed system together. Yet defining outcomes and how best to dedicate staff to achieve them is no easy task, in part because precise calculations of future outcomes are subject to many external factors and unexpected circumstances.

Recommended Solutions

- Engage in a citywide and agency-by-agency review of outcome goals, which should include outreach to and inclusion of stakeholders (citizens, businesses, organizations).

- Create or modify existing performance metrics based on the review. This task will be best accomplished when agencies appoint data/stat liaisons to coordinate efforts.

- Be willing to support programs that show progress toward the outcome metrics and to withdraw from those that don't (for example, what do the numbers show for whether drug therapy or domestic violence intervention better reduces homelessness for a certain population?).

- Measure the time it takes to accomplish activities and the consequences in terms of satisfaction and cost. To recognize and reward speed and customer satisfaction, delayed performance should not carry the same score as timely performance.

The UX Orientation Challenge

Bureaucracies naturally tend to conduct business in isolation, creating forms or programs narrowly based on their own, albeit well-intentioned, perspective. Local government is typically Balkanized, not staffed to consider the efficacy of its communications, and/or indifferent to how its programs are perceived by constituents. In every way, government needs to pivot programs, policy, and service delivery toward UX.

Recommended Solutions

- Incorporate design strategies in all aspects of public interaction (whether bricks and mortar or online).

- Encourage administrators to engage with residents (through interviews or possibly shadowing them while engaged with services) to learn their goals, preferences, and pet peeves.

- Establish a citywide UX department or staff that agencies can or must use for review of signage, websites, forms, and other communications with the public to ensure consistency, clarity, and ease of use.

- Insist on well-publicized customer service outreach at the point of service to constantly capture, evaluate, and publicize citizen satisfaction.

- Adopt an omni-channel approach that allows the citizen to choose the method of public involvement (walk-in, voice call, app/web).

The Technical Challenge

Distributive governance is predicated on City Hall harnessing the capabilities of today's ongoing IT revolution. Unlike existing project innovations in cities across the country, however, the new O/S requires multiple system changes. Technical challenges start with attracting the right talent and include choosing the right software, cleaning and finding data, and establishing protocols for data sharing.

Recommended Solutions

- Establish a data analytics team as a clearly identified focal point for advancing the technical aspects of distributed governance. Require a person in each agency to be the liaison to the team.

- Train agency employees to see presented data as an opportunity to ask "what if" questions for their work and outcome goals.

- Partner with a university to acquire more advanced data science and research skills.

- Require agencies to share data, even if incomplete, unstructured, or duplicative, to force broad improvement in data infrastructure and capabilities.

- Bypass large enterprise implementations in favor of installing cloud-based modules.

- Use imaging and other data tools to stop taking in paper. Legally make the authenticated image, and not the paper form, the document of record.

The Legal Challenge

A host of perceived and real legal issues affect the implementation of the new O/S. Cities face privacy issues about the information they secure from citizens, how they share information among case workers and other employees, and what they post as open data. There are similar, critical issues around security of data, as well as concerns about government use of sensors. These important issues must be addressed head-on at the outset of a new O/S, not after new approaches are adopted.

Recommended Solutions

- Develop operational structures and processes that clarify and codify privacy rules and protocols throughout city government and any agencies that contract with the city.

- Require city auditors to review procedures and results as part of their routine internal audits.

- Appoint a lawyer responsible to the mayor or governor to create an enterprise-wide information-sharing agreement and referee the inevitable inter-agency disputes.

- Institute protocols that include a clear timeline, such as approval or disapproval in ten business days, to resolve situations that are unclear.

- Establish and publish standards concerning how the city collects, protects, and uses sensor-to-sensor data from residents, contractors, and partners using public easements and licenses.

- Begin to establish clear descriptions and legal authorities for major O/S operational reforms and new systems, so they may eventually be codified or enshrined in a city charter revision.

The Risk Aversion Challenge

The new O/S presents opportunities for employees up and down the ranks to exercise more discretion to produce new and effective solutions. That same authority raises the risk of bad decisions. Workers are used to established compliance-based systems that offer an easier path to avoiding mistakes. Media, particularly social media, can amplify a well-intentioned misstep into a very uncomfortable result for the public servant. Workers need to feel confident they will be supported even if every choice they make is not perfect, and they need very clear guardrails and guidance to learn how to advance bold new approaches.

Recommended Solutions

- Clearly and visibly support staff exercising new discretion.

- Encourage risk-taking by employees by measuring results, which allows the city to determine whose production exceeds compliance and reward them.

- Performance reviews should include identifying and rewarding employees who took evidence-driven initiative, regardless of the outcome.

- Create easy-to-use apps that drive clear and customized information to employees. Train employees to effectively access the support and document the informed use of discretion.

- Make it easier to document why a decision was reached; for example, giving a restaurant a warning ticket instead of a citation.

The Context Challenge: Diversity and Community

The new O/S depends on resident input, participation, and perspective. All citizens do not have the same access to new technologies, and those who do may have language and cultural barriers that limit participation. Furthermore, even a city department's genuine efforts to gain a street-level perspective can be victim to research bias and, in certain communities—particularly low-income, immigrant, and African American communities—there can be significant suspicion of government. Yet cities must make the necessary efforts to fully engage all residents.

Recommended Solutions

- Design specific outreach efforts, such as signposts requesting SMS text messages, to increase submission of neighborhood questions and feedback on service delivery.

- Review all public-facing platforms, such as the 311 center, open data displays, and applications designed for the public, for results that are disproportionately related to race, ethnicity, gender, or other characteristics to detect inequity in government services.

- Translate information in open data and 311 into prominent local languages and include machine translation for other languages, as well.

- Include tools that allow communities to manage open data to fit their context and to examine services by geography.

The Procurement Challenge

Public sector procurement is a dense and elongated process that is often antithetical to the dynamic, distributed system of the new O/S. RFPs take too long, contain too many irrelevant technical requirements, do not generally produce innovation, often exclude collaboration, and focus too much on activities and not results. Technology RFPs, in particular, do not match the current speed of technical innovation.

Recommended Solutions

- View procurements as an opportunity to clarify outcomes and goals and to establish cross-departmental collaboration involving senior officials from relevant agencies affecting important issues.

- Make procurements more accessible by limiting the length of procurement proposals with a clear statement of the problem.

- Experiment more frequently with pilot programs that can be implemented rapidly.

- Invite unsolicited ideas from vendors with the understanding that selection may involve a thirty-day "go-shop" at the end, where the city asks other vendors to match the price or idea.

- Establish processes that accommodate the speed of change by more frequently purchasing services instead of items—software as a service, lighting, and not streetlights, as a service.

- Establish standards and design application programming interfaces (APIs) that facilitate third-party app development.

Index

Index

INNOVATIVE GOVERNANCE IN THE 21ST CENTURY

Anthony Saich
SERIES EDITOR

Innovative Governance in the 21st Century-examines important issues of governance, public policy, and administration, highlighting innovative practices and original research worldwide. All titles are copublished by the Brookings Institution Press and the Ash Center for Democratic Governance and Innovation, housed at Harvard University's John F. Kennedy School of Government.

CPSIA information can be obtained
at www.ICGtesting.com
Printed in the USA
FSOW01n1144211017
40167FS